Bound on Earth

"Truly, I say to you, whatever you bind on earth shall be bound in heaven..."

Matthew 18:18 (RSV)

Bound on Earth

A Festschrift for Edmon Lewin Rowell, Jr.

Edited by Marc A. Jolley,
Graydon F. Snyder, and Don Haymes

MERCER UNIVERSITY PRESS
MACON, GEORGIA
NOVEMBER 2006

1400 Coleman Avenue
Macon, Georgia 31207

First Edition.

Books published by Mercer University Press are printed on acid free paper that meets the requirements of American National Standard for Information Sciences—Permanence of Paper for Printed Library Materials.

Library of Congress Cataloging-in-Publication Data

CIP data are available from the Library of Congress

ISBN 0-88146-080-X//978-0-88146-080-3
MUP/H739

For
Lurline Padgett Rowell and Myrna Rowell Jenness,
and
Edmon L. Rowell, Sr. and
Philip Andrew Rowell,
may their memories be a blessing.

Contents

Preface

"Truly, I say to you, whatever you bind on earth shall be bound in heaven..."
Matthew 18:18 (RSV)

In November 2005 the annual AAR/SBL meeting was hosted in Philadelphia, the city of brotherly love. Love was in the air, and Grady Snyder and Don Haymes approached me about doing a festschrift for Edd Rowell. Chances are, if you are holding this book, you know Edd. Doing a book in Edd's honor is both a blessing and a curse.

It is a blessing because no one I have ever worked with has taught me as much about a profession as he has, but more than that, he has aided so many people in publishing their books that a book in his honor is as natural as a pig in the mud.

It is a curse because Edd is the consummate editor, and is without doubt the most meticulous man with a red pencil who ever bled a page. Therefore, to present him with a book that he has not edited is like giving a sword demonstration to Achilles or a humor lesson to Mark Twain. Each would smile at you, say thank you, then, with their respective gifts, destroy you. So, Edd, we did the best we could. Be kind. If it's the thought that counts, then please count this more than it is.

If you do not know Edd Rowell, please take a look at the vita in the back of this book. This will give you only the skeleton of the man. To know him and his talents and his commitments you must know him personally.

He left the pastorate in 1980 to join Mercer University Press, thinking that after a few years he would return to the pulpit. It's ironic that about the time he left the pulpit, a couple of fundamentalists began to take over the Southern Baptist Convention. A coincidence, I am sure.

Edd has been editing books for twenty-seven years at Mercer. The road back to the pulpit was always open, and he became one of the most popular interim ministers in Middle Georgia, but his love of books and his God-given talents kept him at his vocation of an editor.

I first met Edd in July 1995 when I came to Mercer for an interview with the Press. I was employed at Broadman & Holman Academic books at the time. I walked into Edd's office and he said, "You work at Broadman? Did you work on this book?" He pulled out a book on Baptists that was several hundred pages long, had 1/4" margins, and had no index.

"No, I did not work on that," I said, thankful that I had not had a hand in the book's production.

"Well, it needs an index," he snapped.

So much for first meetings. He soon relaxed, and talked to me as if he had known me for ten years.

I started at Mercer that September. In November, we went to Philadelphia for the AAR/SBL meeting. I was Edd's roommate and while there his shoulder began hurting.

Several weeks later, he was diagnosed with multiple myeloma.

At the time, MM patients could expect to live—with luck—two or three years. Now, eleven years later, most people find it difficult to believe that Edd has cancer.

I have never seen a man put so much of his life into what he does as Edd Rowell. But to do it facing such an aggressive cancer is nothing short of heroic.

Of course, Edd would never count it heroic. He would count his success to two things: (1) he has helped the doctors take care of him, and (2) the Grace of God.

For eleven years Edd and I have worked together every day. In that time, the entire length of time of his fight against cancer, no one has seen him as often as I have, with the exception of his wife, Ruth. I have seen him on dark days and I have seen him on sunny days. I have traveled with him from DC to San Francisco. We have taken long car trips and talked about theology, John Wayne, the Korean War, the Southern Baptist Convention, food, our wonderful wives, and books, books, books. We have laughed until the tears poured out and we have cried until the tears ran out.

Who I am today, in part, is due to who Edd Rowell has made me. And I am the better for it.

Note: The title of this festschrift is my idea, sink or swim. I once had a book specially bound in hardcover and the woman who did it cited Matthew 18:18a in the back of the book with a stamp. Edd has helped a lot of people get their book *bound on this earth*, but it is the binding of his life to others that is *bound in heaven*.

Marc A. Jolley
6 August 2006

Foreword

Prolegomena to an Understanding of a Preachin' Editor: Edmon Lewin Rowell, Jr.

I can read writin', said the Fox, but I can't read readin'.

To come to an understanding of Edmon Lewin Rowell, Jr., one must first come to understand "LA" ...that is, Lower Alabama...but that might take a while, and we haven't got that much time, or space, even in this strangely dissembled book. If we are *from* Lower Alabama, then we *might* understand it, if we were given to thinking hard, but if we have never even been there then we might never understand it, and surely we should never explain it, no matter how hard or how much we thought.

We might remember LA, nevertheless, for surely it is memorable. A man once told me that he was married in the Church of Christ in Dixie, Alabama, and when the preacher intoned, "until death do us part," the entire congregation stood as one and responded, "AAAAAAmen!" That wife was long gone, he said, years later, shaking his head ruefully, but he still remembered the wedding vows. LA had made an indelible impression.

Edmon Lewin Rowell, Jr., was born not far from Dixie, in Covington County, near to Andalusia, close on three score and ten years ago. He grew to manhood, in a time before "manhood" was culturally despised, in a place where all humankind might be valued, though they had but few of the treasures of this earth. Surrounded by the love of Daddy (Edmon, 1910–1999) and Mother (Lurline) and Spot (the

Wonderdog) and (most of all) Granny, young Edd—with two *d-d*s and don't you forget it—came soon to understand that all of this earth that we should value most shall also be found in heaven, even the dirt, or some of it.

That's *clean* dirt, Mr. Haymes, clean dirt!

Yes, Mr. Rowell.

Down in the *clean* dirt of Covington County, Lower Alabama, Edd learned from Daddy, a carpenter, to measure twice, and cut once…and always cut on the *outside* of the line. "You can cut a board shorter," Daddy would say, "but you can't cut it longer." He was building an editor, if not a philosopher, one aphorism at a time. Granny, a master of many arts, taught her young man how to hoe cotton and bait a hook and sew a patch on his pants and milk a cow and bake a blackberry pie on a woodstove…and how, on that same woodstove, to make coffee.

On that great woodstove, in her kitchen, at the back of the house, Granny kept a blue, porcelain coffeepot. Her coffee beans came from the store down the road in a burlap sack, and she ground them with a hand-turned grinder. Unlike Daddy, the carpenter, Granny never measured anything (although she *took the measure* of everything), for, after many years, Granny just *knew* "how much." Every morning she poured fresh water from the well into the pot, and after it a handful of coffee.

Pause.

Granny washed the pot every Sunday morning.

Now, if we are sentient and sensible we may recognize, in these odd facts of a life, a parable of American social history. In the 1940s rich people bought their coffee machine-ground to "fine" or "drip" and vacuum-packed in a can or a jar—just a little at a time, for it was dear—while poor people, hardworking and resourceful, like Granny, bought coffee beans in a burlap sack and ground them at home as best they could. In the first decade of the twenty-first century poor people buy their coffee in a can or a jar, while rich people buy coffee beans in a bag and grind them at a home as best they can Although we may now marvel as we contemplate the sheer strength of Granny's brew, we may grasp her intelligence and courage and faith when we consider how we might awaken at daybreak, 'long about Thursday, every muscle and sinew aching after hoeing or picking cotton or following the plow or pulling stumps or washing clothes with a tub and rub board and hand wringer, days on end…and Granny would just throw another handful of coffee in that pot. We need only inhale and that caffeine would fly to our cerebral cortex without passing through our bloodstream…*Bing*! And on Sunday Granny would wash the pot, take the flatiron down from the stove and press her best print dress, and walk to the Zion Rock Primitive Baptist Church, where she would pray for the forgiveness of sins and for the strength to get up and do it again.

Praise the Lord!

Amen, Sister.

Thank you, Jesus!

As God intended, they sang *a cappella* at Zion Rock, and there young Edd Rowell learned *The Sacred Harp*—another discovery of the affluent in the later twentieth century—along with the power of prayer and the sedative properties of the sermon. On other Sundays in Daddy's congregation, Shady Hill Freewill Baptist Church, they sang from Stamps-Baxter and taught from the Bible, and the young man learned both canons from cover to cover. Mother, Sister Lurline, brought her son on two Sundays of every month to Beda Missionary Baptist Church, where he found the Broadman hymnal and Miss Lottie Moon. Once the crops were harvested—the cotton baled and shipped, the tomatoes and snap beans and corn and blackberries and peaches canned, the apples sliced and dried, the hog slaughtered and salted away—then the great revival would begin, with a powerful evangelist, and all the Baptists of Covington County (and even the line-drawing Campbellites and the dry-cleaned Methodists) would come together to praise God and save sinners. What then could the young man become but a lover of the South and its soil, fully a Baptist and fully an ecumenist, a sweet singer of psalms and hymns and spiritual songs, a student and teacher of the Bible, a fervent missionary?

By the time Sergeant Rowell shipped out to Korea in the mid-1950s, the shooting was over, but the tense truce and politics of stalemate had only just begun, along with the rebuilding of the peninsula south of the 38th Parallel. Edd Rowell came to the Army of the United States already a "man" although still a boy, and not only a man but also a marksman, sure of eye and steady of hand. The Army made him a typist, a master of the keyboard who understands the mental as well as the physical process of rapid and accurate "data entry." He emerged typing what he thinks faster than most of us can think, a confluence of skills that would serve him well in Howard College (AB, 1961) and Southeastern Baptist Theological Seminary (BD, 1966), in more than fifty Baptist churches and a couple of Baptist colleges, and surely in Mercer University Press, where, after more than a quarter of a century, Edmon Lewin Rowell, Jr., is a legend still in the making.

In the half-century since his sojourn in Korea, Edd Rowell found the mentors, colleagues, professors, confessors, and authors who populate the pages of this book. They are, each in their peculiar ways, his fathers, mothers, brothers, sisters in faith, and all of them are his intellectual and spiritual progeny. One of them is his daughter in the flesh, the eldest of three children of accomplishment, as grand a combination of her mother and her father as she could be, a daughter and a sister to Edd Rowell in spirit as well. If we know nothing else of Dr. Margaret Elizabeth Rowell McGinnis, we should know that, in addition to all her other achievements, she was once the six-year-old daughter of the Baptist preacher who desegregated her public elementary school in Livingston, Alabama, her father at her side. Then and now Beth McGinnis fulfills her father's lifelong mission "into all the world, beginning here." She belongs in this book. Many more siblings, parents, and progeny in spirit and wisdom belong, and would be here if they could.

Festschriften form a peculiar genre. They are gifts of love, though they be almost inevitably ungainly and often incoherent. At best they enter into conversation with the beloved—bestowing homage, acknowledging debt, declaring independence, breaking new ground, starting an argument. So it is here. It is almost always the disciples and colleagues of a great eminence, vassals and peers, who assemble and offer a *Festschrift* to honor the true *genius* who has taught them, provoked them, nurtured them, and inspired them as their mentor and exemplar. So it is here. It is the students who honor their teacher; this is a natural order. Yet here we find, uniquely—I know only one other case, and a truly strange one—at least one author who is formally the teacher of the student he honors, and Edd Rowell has learned from all the authors in this book as surely as they have learned from him. They continue many conversations with some of their beloved's many passions: editing, the singing of praise to God, the American South, Kierkegaard, the politic arts, Baptists, the missionary church, and the preaching of *good* news. These are offerings of love, what the poet Edna Millay called missionary church, and the preaching of *good* news. These are offerings of love, what the poet Edna Millay called

> Love in the open hand, no thing but that,
> Ungemmed, unhidden, wishing not to hurt,
> As one should bring you cowslips in a hat
> Swung from the hand, or apples in her skirt,
> I bring you, calling out as children do:
> "Look what I have!—And these are all for you."

May the reader find them lovely as well, a worthy introduction and homage to a truly lovely human being. May the Peace of God dwell always with him and with you.

Don Haymes
7 September 2006

Acknowledgments

Thank you to the following:

Grady and Don for suggesting we do this now;

To each contributor who wanted to be a part of this publication;

To Beth who provided much information and was always responsive to my email requests;

To Ms. Ruth for scaring me with a photo of Edd;

To Marsha for her enthusiasm and secrecy in this whole process;

To Kevin for copyediting the book. Few have the professionalism to take care of authors the way Kevin does, but fewer have the guts to copyedit a book in honor of the master;

Jim for designing the cover and not being scared but inspired by the scare;

Finally, to Edd for not knowing what we have been up to. (And if you did know, thanks for not telling us.)

A Personal Tribute

Reading Between the Lines:

An Essay in Celebration of an Edd–itor

JOHN I DURHAM

Too few by half are the patient and painstaking scholar-gypsies who give their minds (and eyes) to the perusal, correction, improvement (and sometimes the creation) of the written words of others. For the most part unsung, the best of them, they are yet the invisible armor of the front-line *professeurs* who gladly publish so that they will not perish from the company of the tenured.

In cloistered corners quiet, these scholar-gypsies labor to save the English language from syntactical devastation. Often, they must give what amounts to literary CPR to manuscripts that are Dead On Arrival. Frequently, they must check "facts" that turn out to be fiction, and now and then they are required to spend a day or two of labor to locate a source that may not even exist.

They are guardians of truth, this fellowship of the blue pencil. To be competent for the task they have embraced, they must be both well educated and even intelligent. They must know what a sentence is, and what a dictionary is for, and that PC spell-checking and style-guiding is too often a bruised reed. They have to be linguists and *savants* and have an acute sense of humor. And most of them, praised may they be, have set aside careers in research and the creativity that research necessitates to give themselves to the background (backroom) work of the editor. They are even sometimes authors unsung.

This essay is a celebration of one of them, an editor called EDD-itor by those who know him and have been made better at what they do by his disciplined and critical eye. I called him once "*Der Herausgeber* of the eagle eye," thanking him for his "gift for patient precision, and the belief that writers, though a trial, are necessary." I was showing off, but my assessment was both sincere and completely accurate.

There are those who would understand his name as acronymic, and they would not be off the mark to do so:

E—edit
D—delete
D—dictionary, forsooth

R—references!!!!!!!!—"for your reference pleasure"[1] [*sic*!]
O—*opera citato*, no no no, nevermore
W—"When in doubt, look it up."[2]
E—"*Elements of Style*, *The*: "plain enjoyment (read, *fun*)"[3]
L—"like" no; "as," yes
L—"larder": birdseed, V8 juice, crackers, beans, applesauce, and peppermints[4]

---

[1] Edmon L. Rowell, Jr., *Footnotes and Others. Mercer University Press Shortguide* (Macon GA: Mercer University Press, 1981-2001, "revised" seven times, "corrected," seven times, "recast" four times).

[2] Ibid., 11.

[3] Ibid., 11.

[4] Ibid., 18n12.

Edd is of course an author as well as an editor, as the bibliography of his writings at the end of this volume will attest. From an op-ed piece in the *Bull Mountain Bugle* (I am not kidding.) in 1969 to his *Finding God in the Rest of the Story* in 1998 and both before and after that period nearly three decades in length, he has taken pen in hand and typewriter and an array of keyboards under fingers, and the result has made us a contribution of a different sort.

Edd is also in fact a translator, and even an emergent artist—long years ago, he translated the Hebrew text of Ezekiel's vision (Ezekiel 1:4–28) then made a drawing illustrating that text, the assignment of a somewhat wild-eyed seminary professor. He has that drawing yet, I suspect, somewhere. He parts not with a single scrap. Never has. Yet.

Then there are his contributions as minister, both resident and "intermittent" pastor, and as hero, in which latter role he has taken on and brought to bay "a noxious thing"[5] that tried to seize him and poured out encouragement to an array of compatriots in treatment. I digress, however—the celebration I want most to make concerns the legacy we have from Edd's work as editor.

There are of course varieties of editorial activity. Having done not a little editorial work myself and enjoyed the slings and arrows of authorial indignation, I can attest the variety of character assassination flung toward editors. I list only a few of them:

> 1. The editor devoid of sensitivity—how could anyone miss the quality and insight in this original work?

---

[5] Psalm 41:9.

2. The editor as vandal—how could anyone presume to suggest the deletion of even a word from this inspired manuscript?

3. The editor as a weapon of mass destruction—how could anyone be so arrogant as to deprive the needful world by rejecting this unique contribution to learning?

4. The editor as ignoramus—who appointed this jerk the judge over a book he/she is not smart enough to understand?

5. The editor as a jealous (read unpublished) author—those who cannot write can only edit.

And so on: the scorned author, even the gently corrected author, sometimes succumbs to a fury second only to the fury of the scorned woman. This scorn usually increases in its intensity in direct proportion to the weakness of the manuscript presented, a case of the greater the editorial pressure the greater the volume of hot air.

The competent editor has of course seen and heard all this and can generally anticipate it in advance by a first quick perusal of any manuscript, however that manuscript may have arrived: under the door, over the transom, in the post with a note from a friend of the author who just happens to be a member of the publisher's board, or even solicited by the editor himself in a moment of delirium.

What, however, is to be said about the editor's task without reference to authorial fallout, the challenge editorial that is in itself daunting enough?

The longsuffering editor must deal with such offerings as the following:

1. The palimpsest manuscript—the work of the author who has written over earlier writing, his/her own or betimes, alas, over someone else's earlier writing. The editor must look behind and over and under and around the lines thus submitted in a search to find something with which to work. Now and then, what lies beneath belongs to someone else, *à la* the infamous Jayson Blair, *et al.* Usually, nothing lies behind the words except blank paper, now wasted. The editor's faith "gives substance to" his/her hopes, and searches for "realities not seen," but most frequently in vain, for only rarely is that faith justified in these cases.

2. The pentimento manuscript—the term is somewhat archly applied by art historians to details in a painting altered and obscured from view by an artist who has changed direction. Such a detail is painted out by being painted over, and the revision takes its place. With passing time, however, overzealous restoration sometimes reveals the original behind the revision, as for example a second left ear for Judas in Michelangelo Merisi da Caravaggio's *The Taking of Christ*, now in the National Gallery of Ireland.[6] With such a manuscript, the editor must "clean away" what may be called the author's overwriting to discover the argument underneath. All too often, naught but disconnected fragments remain when this process has been completed, fragments nonetheless that give a hint at the book that might have been.

---

[6] A fascinating account of the discovery and restoration of this painting has recently been published by Jonathan Harr: *The Lost Painting* (New York: Random House, 2005). For an account of Judas' left ear, see pp. 170-71.

3. The *inter alia* manuscript—here, the editor's job is to read between the lines of the author's submission (not a word authors care for, that) to ascertain what argument may be tucked away amidst all the other sentences and paragraphs (and even chapters). This can be a rewarding undertaking (pun intended), for now and then, there really is content between far too many lines for far too little argument in a manuscript. All too often, however, there turns out to be nothing between the lines, alas.

4. The *kvetch*[7] manuscript—only a Yiddish word will do for this variety of offering, the complaining presentation, the pile of pages that presents in feeble camouflage the axe-grinding whine of congenital bellyacher eager to make "a name" by assault. These offerings are usually quite easy to recognize, but more difficult to deal with, because underneath all the whining hyper-attack there is upon occasion a reasonable and cogent argument. Separating the nut from the shell (or is it the shell from the nut?) can be however an arduous chore.

5. The eureka manuscript—the golden mean, pearl of great price, and El Dorado for which every good editor always hopes. These are the pages that bring joy to the editor's heart, excitement to his/her brain, and occasionally, even a tear to his/her eye. The eureka manuscript has the power to make the editor feel as important as he/she really is, for it comes to hand as an

---

[7] The ultimate and delightful discussion of *kvetch* by Michael Wex, *Born to Kvetch* (New York: St. Martin's Press, 2005), sets forth all anyone will ever need to know about this expressive verb.

almost-book, one the editor will be proud to see published and will even want to own.

Not all authors are suspicious of the editorial hand, and resentful of the editor's effort to make the writer look better than he or she is. The author with any sense understands that it is in the editor's best interest to make any book or article the very best it can be, and is grateful for the advice, the counsel, the learning, and yes, even (sometimes especially) the criticism given, even when it may sting. It is after all the author who receives the royalties, not the editor, and the author who will be pilloried for the gaffes he has made if the editor misses them too.

Nor are all editors equal in talent, wisdom, experience, and sensitive charity. I have myself known as consumer the work of a range of editors, as many perhaps as thirty, at their work in as many as a dozen publishing houses. Most of them have been professional, courteous in their correspondence, eager to be of help, and reasonable in negotiation. Most of them have helped me, a few have amused me, and only a few have made me angry.

Many writers, I do not doubt, will recognize these categories:

1. The silent (sleeping?) editor—the hack who simply passes the work along to be printed. No comment of criticism, no word of commendation, nothing. The manuscript submitted is the work published, warts and all. Period.

2. The sneaking editor—the arrogant would-be who makes alterations in one's manuscript, deletions and even additions that completely change the sense (and

even the fact) of what has been submitted, without any notification of the author, who sees the revisions only in publication.

3. The inept editor—the well-meaning but uninformed or inexperienced "corrector" who follows a rigid grammatico-syntactical pattern that allows no room for variety of expression.

This sort of editing can usually be caught in proof pages, though when no proof pages are offered, the published page with a misplaced (or even an incorrect) "correction" can sometimes be embarrassing and often howlingly funny.

4. The paranoid editor—these individuals, who usually work for repressive bosses frightened of the complaints that may come from what is called "the readership," sanitize the pages that pass into and through their hands to be sure they present no statements offensive to theological doctrine, denominational superstition, political prejudice, patriotic boilerplate, or grandma's accrued wisdom. It matters not whether the statements are documented fact or even necessary to the argument being presented. These bowdlerizations are almost universally made without any notification of the author.

5. The author's editor—caring and care-taking, eager to help and not hinder, with a close eye for details and an encompassing view of the argument as a whole. The author's editor is interested in clarity, accuracy, a congenial style, and above all helping the author to say what he intends to say in a way that is the author's own.

In more than forty years of writing for publication, I have experienced each of these five varieties of editorial attention (and inattention). In some instances, I have enjoyed or endured the work of a whole phalanx of editors on a single piece, involving at least two or even three of the editorial types described above. The experiences that amused and angered me were the result of the work of type four, the paranoid editor.

Many years back, I made reference in a piece interpreting the narrative of the Golden Calf in Exodus 32 to a wonderfully human and humorous painting of the Dutch painter Jan Steen,[8] though with no accompanying reproduction. The piece had a very wide circulation, and one reader complained to the editor, a gentle man and a friend of mine, that Jan Steen was not the artist of the painting by that name. As I was out of the country on sabbatical leave at the time, he made bold to apologize to the reader, noting that "Dr. Durham is usually more careful about these things," and forwarding to me the correspondence.

I much enjoyed acquiring and sending along to this editor the museum's statement of provenance, going all the way back to Steen himself, along with a photograph of a large gourd in the bottom right corner of the painting on which in large letters is the painter's own signature, "Steen" with a "J" drawn through the "S." There are of course any number of paintings on this as on most biblical narratives, and I wrote with a chuckle to my editor friend, "Be careful about confessing my sins until you are sure I have committed them."

The experience that angered me also involved biblical interpretation, this time a treatment of the narrative prologue to the Book of Job. I prepared a somewhat involved discussion

---

[8] This work, *The Worship of the Golden Calf*, painted around 1672, may be seen in the North Carolina Museum of Art in Raleigh, North Carolina.

of *HaSatan*, the "Adversary" whom God sends forth to check on the world's hypocrites, a considerable population. For a variety of reasons, my article went through the hands of more than one editor.

Aware of course that the narrative was a somewhat sensitive one and that "The Satan" has a large number of religious fans, I had exercised considerable care to explain both the story and the role of the Adversary in the theology of the Old Testament. At least one of the editors who worked on the piece apparently thought my explanation prolix, and deleted it almost entirely, leaving a phrase that, standing without qualification, proved so incendiary that the skies fell in.

All this was done without any notification in my direction, and when the inevitable reaction began to roar, the editor's supervisory authority announced to the reading public that the publishers of my piece had no part whatever in the creation of the piece, and that the objectionable interpretation was totally the author's, allowed to slip through by a lax editor. In truth, the editor who made the deletions was not lax enough.

Editors are not perfect animals, anymore than authors are "inspired and without error." Editors have ego, as do the rest of us, though authors in general would prefer that they keep that ego hidden. As for the authorial ego, only mega-terms can adequately describe it—perhaps only preachers and other actors display ego in grander doses. Ego may indeed be an essential part of an author's incentive: why otherwise would anyone believe that what he/she wants to say on a subject is worth saying by way of the unchanging face of a printed page?

The good editor, the professional editor, the editor who just may be born to the task and so made *for* the task must thus therefore be an ego-hider and an ego-scratcher. Such an editor's own ego is satisfied, in professional life by the cultivation, within reason, of the author's ego. Good editorial work will often make the author's words more clear than they were to begin with, the author's argument more telling than it was to begin with, the author's contribution better than it might have been, and all in a cooperative partnership that leaves both editor and author happy with their work.

Edd Rowell is such an editor. He is an author's editor who cares about his writers, and who would never think of changing even a word or phrase significant to an author's argument without consultation. If he feels that his own expertise is inadequate to assess a complicated manuscript, he enlists (with a reasonable remuneration) a specialist to read and appraise the author's effort. I have myself vetted works submitted to him, and I can attest that no comment of mine was passed along to any author without my permission.

Edd's scrutiny of a manuscript is microscopic. His attention to style, precise. His ability to find the best sources, uncanny. His respect for the writer, absolute. His sense of humor, a helpful lubricant for a sometimes sensitive process. His thoroughness in getting things right, unceasing. And he is the single editor of the many with whom I have worked across a great many years to spell my name correctly. He has recorded on the printed title pages "John I Durham," from the very first and thus without the repeated corrections that have in most other instances been necessary (and sometimes ultimately still ignored).

For all these reasons, along with a great many more, Edd Rowell is Mercer University Press's senior editor. In a way, he is Mercer University Press's Everyman: he has been with the Press from the very beginning, has at one time or another done virtually every needful task, from packing (and lifting) boxes to soliciting manuscripts, from moving house to making coffee, from opening shop in the early (*early!*) morning to hawking the Press's printed products at conferences and conventions.

I believe it is not too much to describe Edd Rowell as the soul of Mercer University Press, and in times both good and hard, its anchor. His colleagues may be forgiven for suspecting that he can walk on air; some of us have seen him do it. He brings to the office cheer and good vibrations, and all of us who know him are thankful for such a gift.

I knew Edd first as a student in my seminary classes. Then I knew him as a pastor foolhardy enough to give his teacher the freedom of his pulpit. Then I knew him as a correspondent, then as a Mercer Press staffer, then more than once as my editor. Now I know him as a flagger of e-articles informative, astonishing, and amusing. And all the time I have known him as I know him still, as a friend.

So keep at it, Edd-itor. We who are in your debt are legion, and we thank you for helping us know how to read, and how to write, and to think we did it all by ourselves.

The Academy

The Wind Blows where It Will

Hymnannies, Passion Chorales, and Sacred Jazz

BETH ROWELL MCGINNIS[1]

When I was a child, my father was pastor and my mother the minister of music at the First Baptist Church of Livingston, a West-Alabama town of about 2,500 people plus a university. Periodically on Sunday nights (Sunday-evening services were still alive and well then), my father would hold a "hymnanny," during which members of the congregation would holler out the numbers of their favorite hymns, which everyone would then sing, at least for a verse or two. As anyone who has ever been part of a hymn-singing knows, this process could be quite competitive, with some members eschewing the singing altogether in order to find the numbers they wanted to have sung and be the first to holler next. My favorite hymn at the time was "The Old Rugged Cross," number 430 in the new (1975) *Baptist Hymnal*. I didn't even have to look it up.

I'm not sure what my favorite hymn is now, but it's definitely something more high-church than "The Old Rugged Cross." Maybe "Be Thou My Vision" or "God of Grace and God of Glory" or "Praise to the Lord, the Almighty." I learned

---

[1] Beth McGinnis is the daughter of Edd Rowell. She teaches music at Samford University in Birmingham, Alabama.

to love these hymns when our family moved to Macon, Georgia, and settled at the First Baptist Church there, a place where the choir processes and sings the Rutter Requiem. Years later when I programmed these high-church hymns during a stint as minister of music in a small Baptist church in North Carolina, they met with less than hearty approval. A woman whose father had built the church and who lived, at seventy-eight years old, in the house in which she was born, told me she wanted to sing more of "the old hymns." By this, the woman—I'll call her Flora—meant late-nineteenth to mid-twentieth-century gospel, or anything by Bill Gaither. "Because He Lives," "Victory in Jesus," and certainly "The Old Rugged Cross" all fit the bill. These hymns were usually located in the 300 and 400 sections of the hymnal; anything before the 1930s was suspect except possibly "Holy, Holy, Holy." "A Mighty Fortress Is Our God" was right out. Occasionally I played jazzy hymn arrangements on the piano, and I think Flora put these in the same category as organic farming—of the devil.

Despite my quibble that "A Mighty Fortress" *is* an old hymn, Flora's request was reasonable. Church music is a matter of identity. For nearly seventy-eight years, Flora had sung "the old hymns" at that same church, just as she had brought deviled eggs to dinners on the ground. Identity is no less a force at First Baptist Macon, which, like many other moderate Baptist churches, observes Advent with banners and candles and holds an Easter vigil on Holy Saturday. I remember singing "Low in the Grave He Lay" at Easter sunrise services on the football field in Livingston, followed by breakfasts of country ham and biscuits. (Sunrise services seem less popular in some churches these days. We never had them at First Baptist Macon. I wonder, do moderates just want to sleep later?)

Of course, what side of the Baptist fence you're on is only one of the many identities church music can express. "Low in the Grave He Lay" may mark the boundaries between city and country and past and present as much as it marks any theological boundaries. Another friend (closer to my own age) at that North Carolina church even went so far as to distinguish between church music and Christian entertainment music. In her car, she enjoyed listening to "bebop" music (Christian contemporary, not Charlie Parker), but she thought anything but hymns was out of place in church. She had a scientific rationale for this distinction: someone once explained to her that pop and rock beats were out of sync with the rate of a normal human heart and therefore go against the natural order God created. Hymns are more in tune with our heartbeats and better suited for worship.

Christian contemporary music has both foes and adherents, and not all of the foes are old. Some intellectuals find it difficult to relate to the emotional appeal and repetitiveness of many praise-and-worship choruses. More than once have I squirmed uncomfortably in my pew while listening to a contemporary piece whose pop style conveyed to me nothing more clearly than sexual longing. Surely many good middle-class Christians had similar thoughts in the 1950s when their children listened to blues or early rock on the radio, or in the 1980s when Amy Grant came on the scene.

At the same time that I was learning music ministry with Flora, I was also studying musicology at the University of North Carolina in Chapel Hill. Musicologists have a different take on music than do other people; musicologists debate whether music even *has* any content other than its strictly musical structures. In fact, this question has been called "by far the most pervasive...of music aesthetics."[2] I once told my friend with the heartbeat theory that music had no intrinsic meaning other than musical meaning, and that we only attach other meanings to it through convention. She looked at me as if I had just sprouted antlers.

My friends in that small North Carolina congregation hit on an important truth in their discussions of church music. Downhome and downtown, then and now, music is a way we know God, and a way we know ourselves. In musicology, too, the relationship between religion and music is the subject of ongoing discussion. With much of the Western musical canon that is the main focus of historical musicology, religion was an integral part of the music's original context. To what degree does that religious context impinge on our interpretive process today? For example, with a composer such as J. S. Bach, much of whose music is liturgical, is the historical religious context essential to understanding and appreciating his music? Conversely, the jazz composer Duke Ellington primarily wrote secular music, but late in his career he created three "sacred concerts." Does his secular jazz style have a place in a religious context? The cases of both Bach and Ellington raise questions about the relationship between musical form and extramusical content.[3] Both provide ample opportunity for reflecting on the differences, if any, between sacred and secular music.

In the debate over musical and extramusical meaning, J. S. Bach is the grand prize. In a purely musical sense Bach was a

---

[2] Peter Kivy, "Aesthetics," in *The New Harvard Dictionary of Music*, ed. Don Michael Randel (Cambridge MA: The Belknap Press of Harvard University Press, 1986).

[3] Extra-musical meaning is any content or subject beyond the musical structures themselves, i.e. the notes, rhythms, harmonies, textures, timbres, dynamics, etc.

"supreme arbiter and lawgiver of music, a master comparable in greatness of stature with Aristotle in philosophy and Leonardo Da Vinci in art."[4] However, he is nearly as well known as a devout Lutheran cantor who frequently put religious symbolism, both obvious and obscure, into his sacred and even secular compositions. Bach inscribed scores with "J. J." (*Jesu, Juva:* "Jesus, aid") and "S. D. G." (*Soli Deo Gloria:* "Glory to God alone"). The first page of his *Clavier-Büchlein,* a book of teaching pieces for his oldest son, carries the inscription "I. N. J." (*In Nomine Jesu:* in the name of Jesus). Speaking of thorough bass, the typical manner of Baroque keyboard accompaniment, Bach said that "the aim and final reason, as of all music, so of the thorough bass should be none else but the Glory of God and the recreation of the mind. Where this is not observed, there will be no real music but only a devilish hubbub."[5] Musicologists have pondered the connection between religion and Bach's music at least since the nineteenth century—that is, since there was such a thing as musicology. In a sense, the history of Bach studies is a history of musicology in microcosm. At the heart of the debate is whether Bach's music is to be understood as an expression of devout Lutheran piety or in terms of sheer musical structures, or as something in between.

A number of scholars have found in Bach's music a religious content beyond that of the texts. This extramusical content may transcend or enhance the religious and theological implications of a text, or exist entirely apart from a religious

---

[4] Nicolas Slonimsky, ed., *Baker's Biographical Dictionary of Musicians,* 8th ed. (New York: Schirmer Books, 1992) s.v. "Bach, Johann Sebastian."

[5] Quoted in Hans T. David and Arthur Mendel, eds., *The Bach Reader: A Life of Johann Sebastian Bach in Letters and Documents,* rev. ed. (New York: W. W. Norton & Company, 1966) 33.

text. There are almost as many ways to understand the connection between religion and music in Bach as there are authors who write about it. One of the most common concepts is tone painting, in which a musical figure bears a metaphorical resemblance to an idea in the text, for example a rising melodic line with text about ascent. Bach also occasionally painted a more abstract tone picture to set the word "cross." The melodic line would cross over itself by either ascending or descending, and then going farther in the opposite direction. Bach's musical setting of his own name, the famous B-A-C-H motive, does just this: the motive descends from B-flat to A, then reaches up past B-flat to C and back down to B-natural.[6]

Many instances of tone painting involve transferring to music the rhetorical *loci topici*, words or phrases that describe states of physical movement, rest, or position (e.g. "run," "ascend," "descend," "heaven," "mountain," etc.). Manfred Bukofzer labeled this sort of connection "allegory," the distinguishing characteristic of which is coherence between sign and meaning; musical descent corresponds to physical descent. David Schulenberg has disputed Bukofzer's typology, pointing out that "a spatial-kinetic quality such as 'descent' cannot be literally present in a musical figure." The connection between physical descent and the musical figure is already metaphorical; to claim that a descending melody allegorizes the word "descent" in a text is to layer one sign on top of another. This interpretive process becomes more problematic as the number of layers increases, since the level of abstraction also increases.[7]

---

[6] In the German musical alphabet Bach used, "B" corresponds to B-flat and "H" to B-natural.

[7] Manfred Bukofzer, "Allegory in Baroque Music," *Journal of the Warburg and Courtauld Institutes* 3 (1939–1940): 3; David Schulenberg,

Other interpretations involve signs that are more abstract or that operate at a deeper structural level of music, for example modulations between keys. Eric Chafe has ascribed theological import to the modulations in Bach's passions and cantatas. Typically, keys with more sharps have more positive affective associations than do keys with more flats. Thus Chafe sees flatward modulations and minor keys in Cantata 77, "Du sollt Gott, deinen Herren, lieben" ("Thou shalt love the Lord thy God") as expressive of the discouragement that can result from awareness of God's law and human inability to follow it. Another kind of abstract sign is numerological; Friedrich Smend and others have used cabalistic techniques to decode intricate numerological systems in Bach's music.[8]

Some writers have drawn analogies between musical form and social or philosophical structures. In Susan McClary's analysis of the fifth Brandenburg Concerto, the flamboyant harpsichord cadenza is the act of an individual asserting herself against a dominating group. Michael Marissen also considers the Brandenburg concertos analogous to social structures, but sees those structures through the rubric of Lutheran belief about social hierarchies: such hierarchies reflect divine order in the world but do not represent the ultimate reality of the

---

"'Musical allegory' Reconsidered: Representation and Imagination in the Baroque," *The Journal of Musicology* 13/2 (Spring 1995): 214–15.

[8] Eric Chafe, *Tonal Allegory in the Vocal Music of J. S. Bach* (Berkeley and Los Angeles: University of California Press, 1991) and *Analyzing Bach Cantatas* (New York: Oxford University Press, 2000); Friedrich Smend, "Die Johannes-Passion von Bach. Auf ihren Bau untersucht," in *Bach-Studien: Gesammelte Reden und Aufsätze*, ed. Christoph Wolff (Kassel: Bärenreiter, 1969) 11–23, 153–75, 176–94. Ruth Tatlow amassed considerable historical evidence in debunking Smend's theory, at least where it concerns number alphabets. See Tatlow, *Bach and the Riddle of the Number Alphabet* (Cambridge: Cambridge University Press, 1991).

kingdom of God. Accordingly, the structure of the orchestra is a microcosm of secular but God-ordained social hierarchies. Occasionally, however, Bach disrupted these hierarchies, for example by reversing conventional solo and accompanying roles, thereby offering a glimpse of equality in the world to come.[9]

To be meaningful, this analogy of Marissen's depends upon another method of connecting music and the extra-musical: conventional associations. At my North Carolina church, Flora associated jazz rhythms and harmonies with Saturday night and sin. Bach's contemporaries also learned common associations between music and extra-musical content, and Marissen maintains that today's audiences will not fully understand Bach without an appreciation of those contemporary associations. Unless an audience considers violas and cellos to be orchestral accompanying instruments and violas da gamba to be solo instruments, the reversal of roles in the sixth Brandenburg concerto has little meaning. Listeners learn associations such as these through their repeated occurrence in a repertory, and also within a work by repetition. For example, after hearing Christ repeat the words *Ich bin's* ("I am he") or similar text to the same cadence several times in the *St. John Passion*, listeners can associate Peter's denial with Christ's

---

[9] Susan McClary, "The Blasphemy of Talking Politics during Bach Year," in *Music and Society: The Politics of Composition, Performance and Reception*, ed. Richard Leppert and Susan McClary (Cambridge: Cambridge University Press, 1987) 13–62; Michael Marissen, *The Social and Religious Designs of J. S. Bach's Brandenburg Concertos* (Princeton: Princeton University Press, 1995).

affirmation of his own identity when Peter denies Christ to a similar cadence.[10]

Marissen, Chafe, and others strive to illuminate these historical associations for today's audiences, but other writers focus on methods of interpretation that do not transfer as well to the current day. These writers are more interested in what the music *meant* than what it *means*. Some historicist interpretations explain the relationship between Bach's music and the extra-musical in terms of the Baroque doctrine of the affections, the belief that music could arouse states of the soul such as love, hate, anger, and fear. Other interpreters have attempted to reconstruct the historical view that music reflects the harmony of the cosmos.[11] Robin Leaver has found in Bach's passions the same five rhetorical elements often present in Lutheran sermons: *exordium* (introduction), *propositio* (key statement=biblical text), *tractatio* (investigation of the *propositio*= exposition of the biblical text), *applicatio* (application), and *conclusio* (final statement). Besides rhetorical analysis, Leaver's comparison utilizes several other methods of connecting music and the extra-musical. He relies on common associations to explain introductory and concluding functions, the abstract symbolism of axial symmetry to show how Bach pointed out

[10] See Michael Marissen, *Lutheranism, Anti-Judaism, and Bach's "St. John Passion" with an Annotated Literal Translation of the Libretto* (New York: Oxford University Press, 1998).

[11] See Joyce L. Irwin, *Neither Voice nor Heart Alone: German Lutheran Theology of Music in the Age of the Baroque*, American University Studies series 7, Theology and Religion, vol. 132 (New York: Peter Lang, 1993); Leo Schrade, "Bach: The Conflict Between the Sacred and the Secular," *Journal of the History of Ideas* 7 (1946): 151–94; Philipp Spitta, *Johann Sebastian Bach: His Work and Influence on the Music of Germany, 1685-1750*, trans. Clara Bell and J. A. Fuller-Maitland (London: Novello, 1951); and Christoph Wolff, ed., *Die Welt der Bach Kantaten*, 3 vols. (Stuttgart: Bärenreiter, 1996).

the main focus in an exposition, and Bach's simple musical settings and red lettering for Gospel texts as illustrations of the *propositio* function of presenting the text in a clear, straightforward manner.[12]

Another historicist method is the application of a medieval and early-modern biblical hermeneutic to the interpretation of Bach's music. The fundamental framework of medieval exegesis, still prominent in Reformation biblical interpretation though altered to reflect reformers' theological concerns, was the quadriga, or fourfold sense of biblical meaning: (1) the literal sense or the text as it presents itself, (2) the tropological or moral meaning—what should be done, (3) the allegorical or spiritual meaning—what should be believed, and (4) the anagogic or eschatological meaning—what should be hoped for. Eric Chafe, in an attempt to model the spirit of this hermeneutic and what he believes to be a characteristically Lutheran love of layered and hidden meanings, interprets Bach's music according to various levels of meaning ranging from the concrete textual and purely musical levels to abstract theological symbolism.[13]

A final historicist approach connects music and theology or religious experience by virtue of the intended function of the musical work. For Martin Petzoldt, Bach's passions function as preaching, teaching, liturgy, and theology. Renate Steiger refers to Luther's views of music in claiming that music and preaching have the same function in worship. Jaroslav Pelikan applied an Eastern-Orthodox theology of icons to his understanding of liturgical music: the congregation reaches for

---

[12] Robin A. Leaver, *J. S. Bach as Preacher: His Passions and Music in Worship*, Church Music Pamphlet series, ed. Carl Schalk (St. Louis MO: Concordia Publishing House, 1984).

[13] See Chafe, *Tonal Allegory*.

God through music, and God reaches back through grace. Music is a means of invoking the divine presence, but nothing inherent in the music accomplishes this; the intention of the congregation is key.[14] In addition to theorizing the function of liturgical music as a dialectic between the reach of music and the reach of grace, Pelikan also compares the dual nature of Christ to that of church music: "As praise of the eternal God, Christian art was an expression of boundless freedom; but as the praise of the God who had limited himself in the incarnation, it bound itself to form." For Pelikan, this dialectical nature of church music allows it to transcend its "primarily programmatic function in relation to the text."[15]

In contrast to historicist methods of interpretation, some writers have appealed more to aesthetic theories prevalent in their own time. One example is idealism, which dominated Bach studies from the late nineteenth century into the mid twentieth. Throughout the nineteenth century, the issue of absolute music—music with no explicit connection to verbal or other extra-musical meaning—was at the forefront of musicology. Earlier, instrumental music had occupied a place of lesser status than texted vocal music. Instrumental music was functional as a pleasing background to other activities and it

---

[14] Martin Petzoldt, "Bachs Passionen als Musik im Gottesdienst," in *Johann Sebastian Bach Johannes-Passion BWV 245: Vorträge des Meisterkurses 1986 und der Sommerakademie J. S. Bach 1990*, ed. Ulrich Prinz, vol. 5 (Stuttgart: Internationale Bachakademie, 1993) 44–61; Jaroslav Pelikan, *Bach Among the Theologians* (Philadelphia: Fortress Press, 1986); Petzoldt, "Bachs Passionen"; Renate Steiger, ed., *Theologische Bachforschung Heute: Dokumentation und Bibliographie der Internationalen Arbeitsgemeinschaft für theologische Bachforschung 1976-1996 Mit 15 Textbeiträgen* (Glienicke/Berlin and Cambridge, MA: Galda + Wilch Verlag, 1998).

[15] Pelikan, *Bach Among the Theologians*, 121, 125.

was useful for dancing or entertainment, but it could not communicate meaning in the way that texted music could.

Around the turn of the nineteenth century, a group of German writers began to elevate the status of instrumental music by connecting it to a philosophical ideal realm.[16] For these writers, instrumental music's lack of explicit verbal meaning was an asset rather than a detriment; without specific extramusical content, this music could have universal appeal. Musical structures could express or even manifest spiritual forms through isomorphism, and could thrust listeners into the realm of the Kantian sublime. Throughout the nineteenth century, the debate over absolute music was central to music aesthetics and involved many prominent musicians. Richard Wagner, for example, coined the term "absolute music" and used it pejoratively to indicate a lack of substance and groundedness.

This nineteenth-century debate heavily influenced early Bach studies. Bach's nineteenth-century biographer Philipp Spitta believed that absolute music could invoke the extramusical absolute by reflecting the order and harmony of the universe. Because of this belief, Spitta went to great lengths to defend the purely musical qualities of even Bach's texted church music. In Spitta's construction, Bach's "unalterable" Lutheran chorale melodies and the dictates of strictly musical form elevated Bach's vocal music to the status of pure instrumental music—an expression of the sublime.[17]

---

[16] Notably E. T. A. Hoffmann, Wilhelm Heinrich Wackenroder, and Ludwig Tieck. See Evan Bonds, "Idealism and the Aesthetics of Instrumental Music at the Turn of the Nineteenth Century," *Journal of the American Musicological Society* 50 (1997): 387–420.

[17] Spitta, *Johann Sebastian Bach*.

Spitta's biography has had further implications for interpreting the connection between Bach's music and religion. Determining the correct chronology of Bach's works and drawing conclusions from this chronology has been a pivotal project in Bach studies. From Spitta's biography until the mid-1950s, Bach scholars generally accepted the chronology Spitta established via watermark and handwriting evidence. Spitta's method was generally sound, and produced a chronology that provided the skeleton for Spitta's teleological narrative of Bach's career: over the course of Bach's life he matured from organist to composer of church music to Lutheran cantor par excellence. The Lutheran chorale cantata was the capstone of this development. In Spitta's analysis, Bach adhered most closely to the "sacred and unalterable" chorale texts and melodies in these "late" cantatas, not indulging, as in earlier years, in fanciful embellishments and playful imitations of the melody, but simply surrounding and adorning it. This preservation of the objective, unifying chorale, intact but adorned with subjective "poetic effusions," represented Bach's greatest achievement as reformer of Lutheran church music.

Well into the twentieth century, the academic community accepted both Spitta's dating of Bach's works and his characterization of their purpose. However, in the mid-1950s, Alfred Dürr and Georg von Dadelsen proposed a new chronology, also based on watermark and handwriting evidence along with liturgical information. Their chronology, which remains unchallenged, upheld many of Spitta's findings but also resulted in a few startling revisions, leading some scholars to question Spitta's portrayal of Bach. Most striking was the discovery that a paper type and watermark Spitta had assigned to the 1730s actually dated from 1724–25, Bach's second year in Leipzig. Based on this and other findings, Dürr and

Dadelsen concluded that Bach composed the majority of his Leipzig cantatas in a frenzy of activity during his first few years of residence (1723–26), that nearly all the cantatas preceded 1730, and that after 1730 Bach devoted much more time than Spitta thought to composing and performing secular music. These new conclusions led some scholars to rethink the heretofore accepted image of Bach as devout Lutheran and devoted church musician. Friedrich Blume took Dürr and Dadelsen's chronology as a launching point for interpreting Bach's oeuvre, his disputes with church authorities, and his search for a secular position while in Leipzig as evidence of Bach's dislike of church positions and desire for secular employment.[18] From here the importance of Bach's religious contexts and content diminished in mainstream musicology. Thus the revision of Spitta's chronology marked a turning point in Bach studies, after which theological interpretations have been much less in vogue.

The musicological debate over the interpretation of Bach's music is as much a matter of identity as choosing gospel hymns or praise choruses. Musicians who are themselves religious can identify with religious meaning they find in the music. In my own experience, studying Bach has often been a devotional as much as a scholarly enterprise. Bach's religion is also a ripe field for the kinds of cultural investigations so popular in recent decades. However, religious and other

[18] Friedrich Blume, "Outlines of a New Picture of Bach," *Music and Letters* 44 (1963): 214–17. Also see Adorno, "Bach Defended." For more thorough outlines of these and other major developments in post-World-War-II Bach scholarship, see Gerhard Herz, "Toward a New Image of Bach," in *Essays on J. S. Bach*, Studies in Musicology No. 73 (Ann Arbor MI: UMI Research Press, 1985) 149–84; and Joseph Kerman, *Contemplating Music: Challenges to Musicology* (Cambridge MA: Harvard University Press, 1985) 49–59.

cultural studies of Bach are ultimately secondary, and many scholars prefer to focus on the music itself. They have a point. Few would care about expressions of Lutheranism in Bach's music if the music did not stand on its own merits. As it is, a musicologist can hardly study Bach without eventually having to deal with religion as either text or context.

Such is not the case with Duke Ellington. Ellington was himself religious and he composed sacred music, but one could make a fine career of studying only his secular jazz. With Ellington, the question becomes not (as with Bach) whether his music can be understood *outside* its sacred context, but whether Ellington's music has a place *in* a sacred context. Jazz has strong musical roots in nineteenth- and twentieth-century black religious traditions from preaching styles to spirituals and gospel singing. However, from its earliest days jazz developed a reputation as "the devil's music," the music of Saturday night and sin, corset-check rooms and lascivious dancing. Critics of jazz noted the excessive drinking that commonly went on in jazz clubs and the roots jazz had in blues, a genre whose lyrics can be quite uninhibited when dealing with sexual themes. Some writers even put forth quasi-scientific theories that the syncopated rhythms of jazz (emphasizing the weak beats) stimulated the libido.[19]

Jazz was sometimes referred to as "jungle music," a subtly racist moniker with primitive and sexual connotations. Duke Ellington's band had a regular gig in a Harlem club that played to this racist primitivism. The Cotton Club, where the band played from 1927 to 1932, looked like a large white Southern plantation house. It had a white clientele but hired

---

[19] For example, see Anne Shaw Faulkner, "Does Jazz Put the Sin in Syncopation?," in Rob Walser, ed., *Keeping Time: Readings in Jazz History* (New York: Oxford University Press, 1999) 32–36.

black musicians and attractive Creole female dancers. Ellington's band used sound effects known as jungle sounds, and the club staged elaborate shows built around the jungle theme. These associations with race, primitivism, and sexuality combined to mark jazz in general and Ellington's jazz in particular as music for Saturday night but not Sunday morning. These moral objections to jazz were often a smokescreen for racism and classism. However, not all critics were white; jazz also divided the black community.

So it was with trepidation that Duke Ellington embarked on what was to be his last major project, the three "sacred concerts" that he premiered at Grace Cathedral in San Francisco (1965), the Cathedral Church of St. John the Divine in New York (1968), and Westminster Abbey (1973). As expected, not everyone found the idea of sacred jazz appealing. Before the first concert, someone clipped a promotional *Time* magazine article and wrote across it, "Everything about this concert is disgusting." Ellington and his promoters avoided using the word jazz, tactfully replacing it with "contemporary sacred music." For Ellington, this sacred music was not liturgy—not "the traditional mass jazzed up." Neither was it the same as the secular jazz he played during the week; he saw a difference between playing for worship and playing in entertainment venues such as Harlem's Cotton Club. "One may be accustomed to speaking to people," he said, "but suddenly to attempt to speak, sing, and play directly to God—that puts one in an entirely new and different position."[20]

The difference between Ellington's secular jazz and his sacred music may be primarily functional. Although the music

---

[20] Quotes from Janna Tull Steed, *Duke Ellington: A Spiritual Biography* (New York: The Crossroad Publishing Company, 1999) 120.

has sacred texts and has usually been performed in sacred spaces, it retains many hallmarks of Ellington's secular style, a fact that led jazz critic Gary Giddins to write that Ellington had "brought the Cotton Club revue to the pulpit."[21] A noteworthy example of this juxtaposition of secular style and sacred function is "In the Beginning God" from the first *Concert of Sacred Music.* Throughout this piece runs a six-note melody that signifies the first four words of Genesis, long before the melody combines with text. In fact, Ellington considered every six-note phrase in the entire concert to be symbolic of these six syllables, which are the theme of the concert.[22]

"In the Beginning God" develops this theme extensively through both text and music, which collaborate to compose a theological commentary on the Genesis creation story. An exposition presents the main six-note theme on the piano, baritone saxophone, and clarinet. Following that, the solo singer clarifies the implications of cutting the biblical quote short after four words: "In the beginning God.... No heaven, no earth, no nothing." The speaking choir further elaborates the idea that in the beginning God existed, but nothing else. By chanting the books of the Old Testament, then the New, the choir includes biblical history in the list of things that only came into being as a result of God's creation. Later in the concert, a second version of "In the Beginning God" consists mainly of a solo vocal chant cataloging a long list of items that, unlike God, did not exist in the beginning: "no mountains, no valleys, no main streets, no back alleys, no glory, no gloom...."

[21] Gary Giddins, "At the Pulpit," in *Riding on a Blue Note: Jazz & American Pop* (New York: Oxford University Press, 1981) 160.

[22] Edward Kennedy Ellington, *Music Is My Mistress* (Garden City NY: Doubleday & Company, Inc., 1973) 262–63.

The God of the First Sacred Concert is Thomas Aquinas's prime mover, the "Supreme Being," to quote the title of another Ellingtonian creation account, without whom nothing else would be.

Both text and music of "In the Beginning God" contribute to this theology. In the sectional form of this piece, soloists and ensembles intersperse variations on the main theme with choral chanting. What motivates the structure is the individual color and personality of each instrument or group that takes a turn with the theme. This is par for the course with Ellington, known for his variegated palette of instrumental color and for manuscripts that famously read not "trumpet" or "saxophone" but the names of his band members: "Cootie [Williams]," "Cat [Anderson]," "Harry [Carney]," "Johnny [Hodges]." However, Ellington's customary style takes on specific theological significance in "In the Beginning God." Even before the text paints a sweeping picture of the teeming variety of creation, the musical form embodies that variety. As the text affirms that God is the fount of everything else that is, the music simulates the act of creation with an extended musical form that spins out from one life-giving six-note melody.

Ellington's explanation of the symbolism of the six-note melody, combined with the sacred text of "In the Beginning God," make a theological interpretation plausible. However, the theological content does not change Ellington's signature musical style; rather, the theology works in tandem with the style. Perhaps this is because Ellington believed it was intention, not musical skill, style, or genre, that made music appropriate for worship. "I believe," he wrote, "that no matter how highly skilled a drummer or saxophonist might be, if this is the thing he does best, and he offers it sincerely from the heart in—or as accompaniment to—his worship, he will not be unacceptable because of lack of skill or of the instrument upon which he makes his demonstration, be it pipe or tomtom."[23] For Ellington, a musician's sincerity is what made his offering acceptable.

Bach may have had something similar in mind when he came across a biblical passage having to do with music in worship. Bach used a biblical commentary by the late-seventeenth-century Lutheran pastor and theologian Abraham Calov. For a passage from 2 Chronicles, Calov applied the heading, "How the Glory of the Lord Appeared after Beautiful Music." The passage reads: "It was the duty of the trumpeters and singers to make themselves heard in unison in praise and thanksgiving to the Lord, and when the song was raised, with trumpets and cymbals and other musical instruments, in praise to the Lord, 'For he is good, for his steadfast love endures for ever,' the house, the house of the Lord, was filled with a cloud, so that the priests could not stand to minister because of the cloud; for the glory of the Lord filled the house of God."[24] Bach underlined "Beautiful Music" in Calov's heading and wrote, "N.B. Where there is devotional music, God with His grace is always present."[25] Bach's comment recalls Jaroslav Pelikan's formulation in which the congregation reaches out to God through music and God reaches back through grace. The music's creators, whether composers or performers, do not summon God through form, symbolism, tone painting, or any other device. Rather, the worshippers employ music in the service of devotion and praise, and God responds with God's

---

[23] Ellington, *Music Is My Mistress*, 262.

[24] 2 Chronicles 5:13–14, RSV.

[25] See Robin A. Leaver, *J. S. Bach and Scripture: Glosses from the Calov Bible Commentary* (St. Louis MO: Concordia Publishing House, 1985) 97.

presence. This process runs counter to interpretations based on authorial intent, common even in postmodern musicology. A composer can portray religious themes and can theologize, as in Ellington's "In the Beginning God." But invoking God's presence requires the intention of the worshippers. Without this intention, a performance of even the best religious music is a concert, not worship.

The same is true of hymnannies. When I led hymn-singings at my North Carolina church, I could predict which members would choose which hymns. Flora would call for "Victory in Jesus," another friend for "Because He Lives." My husband would select "Be Thou My Vision" or "It Is Well with My Soul." I always had out copies of *The Broadman Hymnal* (1940), because somebody would surely ask for "Beulah Land" or "Farther Along." We sang these hymns for many reasons: for identity, to remind us who we were, and for history and nostalgia, to remind us who we had been. We sang them to praise God. Sometimes we sang them just for the fun of tapping our feet and harmonizing. It was a nourishing, community-building experience. It fed our souls, and we lived together better as the Body of Christ because of it. And every now and then, worship crept in. It could happen with "Immortal, Invisible" or "Flee as a Bird." The type of music didn't matter; what mattered was that we were there to meet God, and God was there to meet us.

I still believe that musical form has no inherent extra-musical meaning, but the word "inherent" is essential to that statement. Music is rich with extra-musical meanings that are not inherent but that our experience nevertheless has made inseparable from the music. Because of this, there will always be music that is conducive to worship for some but inhibits worship for others. This is also one reason lay participation in worship is important; the intention of the worshippers, not the kind of music performed, is what invites the Holy Spirit. And who knows when or where the Spirit will come? It could be through hymns, cantatas, praise choruses, or sax riffs. The wind blows where it will.

The Meaning of the South

WILLIAM E. HULL

Since the founding of Mercer University Press more than a quarter-century ago, Edmon Rowell has done as much as any editor to put Baptist scholarship in print. At first he worked with a number of university and seminary professors engaged in biblical and theological studies to provide valuable textbooks, monographs, and reference works, notably the *Mercer Commentary on the Bible* and the *Encyclopedia of Religion in the South*. But as the theological education enterprise of the denomination fell into disarray, and as the Press began to gain a wider readership beyond the academy, the focus shifted more to publications on Southern history, culture, and literature in addition to religion and theology. To honor his valuable labors in these areas, I offer Edd one more effort to probe the identity of the region he has done so much to illumine. [1]

Some would question, however, whether there is still a "South" to explain. John Egerton, in *The Americanization of Dixie*, has pointed to leveling forces of mass culture that relentlessly homogenize regional distinctives.[2] Kirkpatrick Sale has analyzed the massive migration of "Yankees" into a once

---

[1] For a recent comprehensive survey in this area see James C. Cobb, *Away Down South: A History of Southern Identity* (New York: Oxford University Press, 2005).

[2] John Egerton, *The Americanization of Dixie* (New York: Harper's Magazine Press, 1974). See also his *Shades of Gray: Dispatches from the Modern South* (Baton Rouge: Louisiana State University Press, 1992).

alien "Sunbelt."[3] At a fiftieth anniversary symposium on W. J. Cash's *Mind of the South* sponsored by Wake Forest University in 1991, Hodding Carter III sounded an epitaph for Dixie because the once binding glue of institutional racism that bonded the Solid South into a segregated society has now been dissolved.[4] For some, the election of Jimmy Carter and Bill Clinton to the US presidency marked the entry of the South into the mainstream of American life, while the enormous influence of Southern religion in the administration of George W. Bush solidified the role of the region as a national power.[5]

But consider: Even if the South is dramatically changing, why the compulsion to explain these changes? Can you imagine anyone preparing an essay on "The New North" or "The Mind of the Midwest," or "The Rocky Mountain Mystique"? Think of the enduring power of the word "Southern" as a modifier, how easily we speak of Southern cooking or Southern women or Southern preaching or Southern accent. Is there any other regional designation with comparable capacity to define?[6] Note how readily we speak of

---

[3] Kirkpatrick Sale, *Power Shift: The Rise of the Southern Rim and Its Challenge to the Eastern Establishment* (New York: Random House, 1975). From 1950 to 1975, the Sunbelt grew from 48,685,000 to 77,651,000, or 59.5 percent, while the rest of the US grew from 102,641,000 to 135,470,000, or 32 percent.

[4] Summarized in Hodding Carter III, "The End of the South," *Time*, August 6, 1990, 82. For his stubborn efforts to preserve a vestige of Southern distinctiveness see "Looking Back," *Southern Cultures* 2/3–4 (1996): 281–93.

[5] Kevin Phillips, *American Theocracy: The Peril and Politics of Radical Religion, Oil, and Borrowed Money in the 21st Century* (New York: Viking, 2006) 97–262.

[6] The closest would be New England, which has lost some of its regional distinctiveness with the decline of Puritanism. For a recent comparative study see Edward L. Ayers and others, *All Over the Map: Rethinking American Regions* (Baltimore: Johns Hopkins University Press,

the Old South or the New South, implying that deep patterns of meaning are superimposed upon the history of this region much like the dispensational ages that Southerners delight to discover in their Scofield Reference Bibles! Who speaks of the Old Mid-Atlantic Region or of the New Great Lakes Region in similar fashion?

No matter how we describe the South, it seems always to be accompanied by an effort to confer *meaning* on the region, as if its identity cannot be understood apart from its significance. In these comments, I shall seek to describe a mindset, an ethos, a lifestyle that is suggestive of the self-understanding shaped by four components of the Southern experience.

I. Place

No one asks "Where are you *from*?" quite like a Southerner. For in the South one *belongs* to a place and does not merely reside there.[7] Southerners were perhaps the original ecologists in the sense that they posited a fundamental bond between person and place, mind and matrix, heart and habitat. In their view, life is profoundly shaped by its setting. As the Apostle Paul explained to the Athenians in good Southern theology, God "allotted…the boundaries of the places where we would live" (Acts 17:26). This sense of one's place as an expression of divine providence tends to make the Southerner more of a realist than an idealist, more of a particularist than a generalist, more of a localist than a universalist. Southerners resonate with

---

1996), especially the contribution by Ayers on "What We Talk about When We Talk about the South" (62–82).

[7] Louis D. Rubin, Jr., *The American South: Portrait of a Culture* (Baton Rouge: Louisiana State University Press, 1980) 7.

the biblical emphasis on a God who is somewhere and not just everywhere. They prefer truth that is concrete rather than abstract. Before deciding on *whither* something is going, they want to know from *whence* it has come.

At the most basic level, this strong sense of place is a response to the physical environment. The earliest explanation of Southern distinctiveness was rooted in the weather. Said William Henry Drayton in 1778, when the South Carolina Assembly was debating ratification of the Articles of Confederation, "From the nature of the climate, soil and produce of the several states, a northern and a southern interest naturally and unavoidably arise."[8] Lest we make light of a factor as commonplace as temperature, let me remind you that the South is full of folks who declined vocational advancement to corporate headquarters in the North because it would involve enduring bitterly cold winters.

Nor can we doubt that the "sunny South" is singularly blessed. "The South is the only region in the United States that fronts the sea on two sides... It has one-third of the good farm land in the nation... It has two-thirds of all the land with 40 inches of rainfall or more... It has a long growing season...[and] is the richest region in renewable resources," possessing in the interior the largest supply of fresh water excluding the Great Lakes.[9] With this plentitude, it is no wonder that a garden myth began to grow according to which the South took unto itself the attributes of the Hebraic Eden

---

[8] Cited by David L. Smiley, "History, Central Themes," in *Encyclopedia of Southern Culture*, ed. Charles Reagan Wilson and William Ferris (Chapel Hill: University of North Carolina Press, 1989) 1109.

[9] Walter Prescott Webb, "The South's Future Prospect," in *The Idea of The South: Pursuit of a Central Theme*, ed. Frank E. Vandiver (Chicago: University of Chicago Press, 1964) 70–71.

and the Hellenic Arcadia.[10] As Jonathan Daniels put it, "We Southerners are a mythological people…who live in a still legendary land."[11]

It was this mythic sense of a Promised Land that prompted the South to define its region as a place to put down roots, to achieve a sense of belonging, and thereby to build enduring structures of community. At the center of this organic linkage stood the family with its "home*place*" that held the clan together. But beyond that were gathering places that nourished an informal networking called neighborliness: the front porch, the town square, the barber shop and beauty parlor, the pool hall, the post office, and, most of all, the church. To be sure, many of these "places in the heart" have disappeared in the hurried pace of modern life, but Louis Rubin reminds us that, even on the busiest Southern interstate highways, good ole boys in their eighteen wheelers happily chatter away over their CB radios and cell phones with anybody who will talk to them, "a splendid, if minor, example of the way in which the so-called Southern life can absorb and humanize even the more recalcitrant and impersonal manifestations of the industrial dispensation."[12]

II. Past

The philosopher Yi-Fu Tuan has pointed out that a sense of place in any society comes from the intersection of space and time. A prime reason why Southerners developed such an acute

---

[10] Lewis P. Simpson, "Garden Myth," in *Encyclopedia of Southern Culture*, 1108.

[11] Cited by George B. Tindall, "Mythic South," in *Encyclopedia of Southern Culture*, 1097.

[12] Rubin, *The American South*, 21.

sense of region was that an unforgettable series of historical events *took place* on that very soil.[13] This legacy enters the Southern mind, not as a fading recollection, but as a living memory. William Faulkner famously remarked that, for Southerners, "the past is not dead; it isn't even past." In this abiding concern for what "came to pass," perhaps the most characteristic phrase in the Bible, we locate the Southern quest for continuity in the midst of change, the respect for tradition that binds together the generations, the innate conservatism that reasserts itself every time those infatuated with tomorrow are tempted to forget the lessons of yesterday.

This concern for legacy is not so much a temperamental bent, however, as it is a sense of faithfulness to those forebears who laid the foundations on which our present life is built. The issue here is one of moral responsibility for preserving and enhancing one's inheritance — and the easiest way to squander that patrimony is to forget it! To those who view this sense of stewardship for the past as mere nostalgia, William Humphrey spoke a corrective in his novel, *The Ordways*:

> We Southerners are accused of living in the past. What can we do? The past lives in us. And not just that single episode which those who accuse us have in mind: the Civil War—but all of the past. If the Civil War is more alive to the Southerner than to the Northerner, it is because all the past is, and this is so because the Southerner has a sense of having been present there

[13] Charles Reagan Wilson, "Sense of Place," in *Encyclopedia of Southern Culture*, 1137–38.

> himself in the person of one or more of his ancestors.... It is with kin, not causes, that the Southerner is linked.[14]

III. Pathos

That the past is, for Southerners, more a matter of family folklore than philosophy of history is seen in the characteristic way that collective memory is mediated through story. Their innate conservatism is grounded, not in some ideological premise, but in a recounted saga. The content of that tale is filled with tragic pathos. It is a story of plantation prosperity stained from its beginning by the "peculiar institution" of slavery. It is a story of valor and courage squandered on a "Lost Cause": the wrong war at the wrong time for the wrong reason. It is a story of deprivation and disgrace in the agonies of Reconstruction and its violent aftermath. If the antebellum South was viewed as a pristine Garden of Eden, the twentieth century gave us a Benighted South savaged, not only by detractors such as H. L. Mencken, but by its own sons and daughters who were merciless in exposing its shortcomings.

Journalists such as Gerald W. Johnson and W. J. Cash reported on virulent racism, religious barbarism, and intellectual sterility. Novelists such as Erskine Caldwell and Thomas Wolfe spat upon the South as a region of poverty, sloth, ignorance, and barrenness. This relentless pounding reached a climax in William Faulkner whose novels were downright frightening in depicting "a South of decaying gentry, idiocy, religious fanaticism, murder, rape, and

[14] William Humphrey, *The Ordways* (New York: Alfred A. Knopf, 1965) 36. By way of example, my mother was named Margaret Jackson King because her father fought with Stonewall Jackson.

suicide."[15] The problem was that historical events repeatedly confirmed his fictional portrayals: the Scopes trial of 1925, the Al Smith presidential campaign of 1928, the Scottsboro case of the 1930s, and the civil rights protests of the 1960s. As Walter Hines Page once observed, the story of the South seems to resemble a ghost story, for always lurking in the background are the ghosts of the Confederate dead, the religious fanatics, and the white supremacists.[16]

In the 1970s, commentators began to deliver the South from its fatal embrace with tragedy. Reputable scholars discovered a progressive dimension in portrayals of the South as its writers escaped the shadow of Faulkner and his view of the region as a tortured land.[17] But this deliverance was short lived. In the 1980s and '90s, militant fundamentalism reasserted itself in strength, racism again reared its ugly head, Jimmy Carter fell into political disfavor, the "New breed" of Southern governors stumbled badly, Wendell Berry wrote the requiem for a dying agriculture, and many turned to the fiction of Flannery O'Conner who found the real South lurking somewhere in the grotesque.

We dare not neglect the economic dimension as a driving force in shaping the troubled Southern psyche. Plantation prosperity and Reconstruction poverty helped form the nineteenth-century mind of the South. This same dialectic reasserted itself in the early twentieth century as the "New South" of Henry Grady struggled with the tenant farmer South

---

[15] Fred Hobson, "Benighted South," in *Encyclopedia of Southern Culture*, 1101.

[16] Cited in Monroe Lee Billington, *The American South: A Brief History* (New York: Charles Scribner's Sons, 1971) 421.

[17] Diane Young, "Telling About the South," *Southern Living*, January 1988, 70.

of Erskine Caldwell. In the late twentieth century, the focus of hope was on the South's thriving cities, especially Atlanta, Charlotte, and Orlando. But what of the rural countryside where the work of yeoman farmers for generations is now covered in kudzu? What of the host of once-stable county-seat towns that threaten to become leaderless as their brightest youth go off to college and never return? What of a "Split-level South" such as in Edd's and my home state of Alabama where seven counties flourish and sixty counties languish in economic stagnation?

In reflecting on Southern hopefulness, the historian F. Nash Boney concluded, "Yet just beneath the gloomy surface of contemporary America, the old optimism still lives in the Southern heartland...the South is stirring again...as Southerners mass for another assault up Cemetery Ridge.... This time the enemy, nebulous but real, is a jumble of obsolete customs and traditions from a past era..."[18] But even a vibrant buoyancy can easily collapse, as George B. Tindall warned in responding to Boney's optimism. "Secessionists, reconstructionists, populists, Wilsonians, Lyndon Johnson, the civil rights leaders, all tended to turn sour when they failed to produce the instant millennium... As the South begins to cast off the burden of Southern history, it will do well to contemplate the memory and—in its headlong rush to the future—not to forget that a heedless optimism can nurture the seeds of tragedy."[19]

---

[18] F. Nash Boney, "The South's Peculiar Intuition," *Louisiana Studies*, cited in George B. Tindall, "The Resurgence of Southern Identity," in *The American South: Portrait of a Culture*, ed. Louis D. Rubin, Jr. (Baton Rouge: Louisiana State University Press, 1980) 166–67.

[19] Tindall, *The American South*, 168.

IV. Piety

With so much pathos in the Southern soul, it is little wonder that its people take their religion seriously, especially a concern for personal salvation with emphases on supernaturalism, revivalism, and emotionalism. Some see this dominant evangelicalism as ethically escapist and socially irrelevant, but for many Southerners it offers a way to rid themselves of what British historian Denis Brogan called the *damnosa hereditas* of the South,[20] that fateful legacy of guilt and shame that comes from living in a Paradise lost somewhere east of Eden. If Christianity can provide catharsis and consolation for the spectral fears that haunt the Southern imagination, then the more of it the better!

For much of its history, the South has served as the dark side of the American soul, a place where sin and judgment could be confronted openly. After all, here was a region stained by the tragedy of racism, a place of suppressed violence that might erupt as a lynching in the heat of the night, a battlefield where the immemorial conflict between good and evil was reenacted again and again. In one sense, the civil rights struggle of the sixties was an acted parable of American redemption and the South was the modern Golgotha where the awful price was paid. In this great travail that was birth-pangs of a better day, the South vicariously sinned for a nation too sophisticated to believe in sin, it vicariously repented for a nation too fastidious to believe in repentance, and it may yet vicariously rise again for a nation too complacent to admit that it is spiritually lifeless.

---

[20] Cited by Tindall, *The American South*, 165.

Many despise Southern religion for its dogmatic fundamentalism, its harsh judgmentalism, its brittle authoritarianism. In a phrase popularized by Will Campbell, they reject it as "Redneck Religion." For them, it is a movement of peckerwoods, ridgerunners, and woolhats willing to be whipped into a frenzy by pulpit demagogues, to stamp their feet in approval of simplistic slogans that clarify nothing, to pass resolutions that would compel the clock to stand still, make their enemies simply vanish into thin air, and leave behind a world for them to remake to their hearts' desire. Some can see nothing in it but bigotry masquerading as piety and they are far more contemptuous of redneck "true believers" than they ever were of Christianity's "cultured despisers." For many thinking people, Southern religion will be the last obstacle to accepting the South as a legitimate member of the American family.

But is this the only way to understand Redneck Religion? Campbell reminds us that the story of Southern rednecks is in many ways as tragic as that of Southern blacks.[21] Languishing in the indentured servitude of the tenant farmer, rednecks lacked the culture that blacks created out of their plantation slavery: they did not even have spirituals to assuage their misery. Driven by poverty from the farms to the mills, working without protection of enlightened laws or labor unions, ignored by the gentry on "the other side of the tracks," they found in their informal, autonomous churches the one place where they mattered, where they could control their destiny, where they could express their resentment of a political and economic system in which they had no voice. Yes, they hated the "Establishment" churches that were run by middle-class

---

[21] Will D. Campbell, "The World of the Redneck," *Christianity and Crisis*, May 27, 1974, 111–18.

"Moderates" who would not give them the time of day. Yes, they yearned for ways to move from the margins to the mainstream of society, and if religion would help them in that quest then by God, they would commit themselves to its stern preachments in order to fight every foot ever laid on their red necks to "keep them in their place."

Perhaps Campbell was right in suggesting that there is more than one kind of racism, and that rednecks are fighting back, in the very same way that blacks did before them by using their religion as the catalyst for systemic social change. If so, then the titanic struggles underway in most denominations, especially Baptist, may be part of that agelong effort to resolve what Gunnar Myrdal called "an American dilemma,"[22] the struggle to accord every race and class a place in the sun with the freedom, dignity, and opportunity that belongs to the children of God. If Southern religion can finally figure out how to redeem both the rednecks and their brothers and sisters in pain, the blacks; if it can learn to embrace them as full members of the family of God; if it can let the Lamb of God take away, not just the respectable sins of the middle class, but the terrible burden of Southern history as well, then it will have made its greatest contribution to the common faith that all America was founded to express.

Here, then, are four ingredients that help us to understand the meaning of the South: a favored place, a remembered past, a tragic pathos, a fervent piety. And what it all adds up to is ambiguity, irony, and paradox. We may say of the South what Winston Churchill said of Russia, "a riddle

---

[22] Gunnar Myrdal, *An American Dilemma: The Negro Problem and Modern Democracy* (New York: Harper, 1944).

wrapped in a mystery inside an enigma."[23] It is the puzzle of a South both old and new, both affluent and destitute, both confident and frustrated, both resourceful and resigned. As Robert Coles put it, "I wonder where else in this country past history and present social conflict conspire to bring forth so much of the evil in people, so much of the dignity possible in people, so much of the 'pity and terror' in the human condition."[24]

The anguish of being a Southerner is perhaps best seen in its expatriates. It is so hard to leave the South, and yet it seems equally hard to return. Willie Morris, for example, made the trek from Yazoo City, Mississippi, to New York City to become, at age thirty-two, the youngest editor in the long history of *Harper's Magazine*, yet he had to write about it in *North Toward Home*. But then, when he was drawn ineluctably back to his roots at the height of racial tensions, fearing that some awful fate would befall him as a liberal Yankee traitor, he had to write about that as well in *Yazoo*, a poignant effort to find himself again and give wings to the oppressive weight of memory. Reflecting on this odyssey of a tortured soul led Morris to express the ambivalence that lurks in the heart of every true Southerner: "I have often pondered what it was that brought me back to stay. I am forever drawn to the textures, the echoes, the way things look and feel… The South is a blend of the relentless and the abiding for me, and an accumulation of ironies so acute and impenetrable that my vagabond heart

---

[23] Winston S. Churchill, broadcast on October 1, 1939, cited in John Bartlett, *Familiar Quotations*, 13th edition (Boston: Little, Brown, 1955) 868.

[24] Robert Coles, *Farewell to the South* (Boston: Little, Brown and Company, 1972) 36.

palpitates to make sense of them."[25] Here we have the hallmark of true Southerners: those who never quit struggling to make sense of their South.

[25] Willie Morris, "Does It Still Exist?," *Southern Magazine*, October 1986, 43.

Toward a Kierkegaardian Politics

ROBERT L. PERKINS

It is now recognized that Kierkegaard was at least minimally socially aware, but that he thought seriously about a few central sociological facts and political concepts and that he was also knowledgeable of some of the dynamics of modern politics in a perceptive though non-professional way are still not widely appreciated. One difficulty readers face when approaching Kierkegaard is that he is self-consciously a dialectical thinker, and any analysis of his thought or terminology that neglects this characteristic will be, at best, misleading. Much attention has been given to his concept of the individual, and properly so, but that he even thought about the political dimensions of his life and times has largely escaped notice until recently.

I propose first of all to present a brief account of the limits Kierkegaard imposed on his authorship and how they required him to abstain from active participation in politics and making application of his thought to concrete social and political issues until the beginning of the attack literature. To support this claim I shall first briefly contrast his understanding of his vocation with his reflections on the nature of the state. I shall then examine three concepts central to the authorship: the political, the numerical, and communication, in order to show how they that lead directly into the heart of his reflections in the late journals on the politicizing of Christianity but not to the Christianizing of politics. To elucidate these concepts it is dialectically necessary to do so with continual reference to "the single individual."

By the time he finished his dissertation, his life-plan seems to have been to become a Christian writer, though his authorship's unity can be understood only after the fact (PV, 5–6). Those who object to this self-interpretation are hard pressed to find an alternate immanent theory to define his life's work.[1] He once considered becoming a police official, an occupation in which he had some interest and for which he thought he had some talent (JP, 4:4946), but he laid that aside. So far as I am aware, that passing thought was the only consideration he ever gave to a life of public service. Moreover, his earliest views of politicians demonstrate a decisive difference between his own intellectual tastes and those of a leading liberal politician of his time.[2]

Although Kierkegaard's perception of politicians remained rather acid (JP, 4:4085, 4092, 4093), his view of "politics" is that it "is egotism dressed up as love" (JP, 4:4206). He realized that there was no political means of reforming Christianity (JP, 4:4208), for the latter was a matter of inwardness and was heterogeneous to the means and ends of the state. Kierkegaard understood and rejected the utilitarian view of the state: it is "egotism in great dimensions, very

---

[1] On recent debates concerning Kierkegaard's vocation and the significance of *Point of View* and other such self-explanatory works see Sylvia Walsh, *Living Poetically: Kierkegaard's Existential Aesthetics* (University Park PA: Pennsylvania State University Press, 1994) 10–15. References for the sigla appear as at the end of the essay in the sequence of their first appearance.

[2] EPW, 6–53. See also Robert L. Perkins, "Power, Politics, and Media Critique: Kierkegaard's First Brush with the Public Press" in *International Kierkegaard Commentary: Early Polemical Writings*, ed. Robert L. Perkins (Macon GA: Mercer University Press) 27–44.

expediently and cunningly composed so that the egotisms of individuals intersect each other correctively," and offered this appraisal as a reason also to reject Hegel's view that the state has "moral significance" (JP, 4:4238). Clearly he agreed with Marx (who is never named) that religion has been and can be used "in order to tranquilize people and thus be better able to rule them," thus nailing down his religious objection to "the Christian state." But there is more: the union of the church and the state leads also to the ruination of the state (JP, 4:4242)! Politics deals with only the finite and temporal, but Christianity is inwardness and cannot be used as a political tool (JP, 4:4191, 4193). The narrowness of the state's mandate clarifies Kierkegaard's objection to voting, which has to do only with the finite: "All finite matters are suitable for voting. Nothing infinite can be decided by voting. A decision by voting means only that the matter has a terminal point, that it is now decided" (JP, 4:4199). This distinction reinforces Kierkegaard's democratic proclivities.

Although only individuals can be politicians, Kierkegaard's concept of the individual has provoked criticism, usually because the concept is treated undialectically.[3] The criticism grows more shrill when the individual referred to is a religious person. For instance, the "witness" is one of Kierkegaard's decisive subcategories of "the individual," for to witness "in God's name" does not mean that "everything must

---

[3] With reference to this issue in Martin Buber, Mark C. Taylor, and H. L. Martensen, see my introduction to *International Kierkegaard Commentary:'Two Ages*, xiii–xxi, and, focusing singly on Buber, see "Buber and Kierkegaard: A Philosophic Encounter" in *Martin Buber: A Centenary Volume*, ed. Haim Gordon and Jochanan Bloch (KTAV Publishing House, 1984) 275–304.

go his way, yield to him, that (the witness) must be capable of everything—ergo, it is wonderful to be such a person... This is the human way of thinking, which at its maximum always wants to make the divine the superlative of the human" (JP, 4:4949). Witnessing is certainly an individuating act, but as the language of success, yielding, capability, and social approval used above indicates, Kierkegaard well understood that even, or especially, a witness on behalf of the otherness of the divine occurs in a linguistic and historical community and stands in dialectical tension with the concept of the divine understood as the summation and justification of human desires.

From an entirely different approach, Kierkegaard, under the guise of Johannes Climacus, argues that the "subjectively existing thinker," the central character in *Concluding Unscientific Postscript to 'Philosophical Fragments'*, is so focused upon his or her own task of becoming subjective that others are set free to accomplish the same in the common world everyone shares (CUP, 1:74, 80). The social import of such a position is clear: the subjective existing thinker is at the top of no social, political, religious, or any other kind of hierarchy and is certainly no elitist, for every human being has the same task (CUP, 1:247–49). Since becoming subjective is the universal task facing every person, it is defined differently in every clime and culture. The varieties of the subjective truths to which persons are devoted suggests that some of these are in contradiction with others and such difference cannot be checked by appeal to a fact. Of course, subjective existing thinkers who make contrary claims may both be wrong, though only one can be correct.[4] This contrariety of competing

[4] See Robert L. Perkins, "Habermas and Kierkegaard: Religious Subjectivity, Multiculturalism, and Historical Revisionism"

subjective truths is more than merely logical; it also creates a political and social world.

Political philosophy and practice are complex combinations of both subjective and objective or publicly debatable truths. Being a "liberal" or a "conservative" is immensely complicated and goes to the deepest roots of character. Character is nourished and/or poisoned by experience, in the widest possible sense of that term, and finally chosen and formed in the complex trivia and crises of life. These political acts of the single individual create communities and make politics possible and necessary. The single individual "is dialectically decisive as the presupposition for forming community… The cohesiveness of the community comes from each one being a single individual, [for] [e]very single individual guarantees the community" (JP, 3:2952). Individuals such as Kierkegaard describes are politically essential to the good health of the political, be that politics liberal or conservative. Reminiscent of Plato, the isomorphism of the individual and the community is achieved, and "in a good sense…*unum noris, omnes*" (JP, 3:2952; "If you know one, you know all.").[5] But all is not well in the actualization of this idealized world. According to Kierkegaard, subjectivity and, along with it, politics are subverted in contemporary life.

International Philosophical Quarterly 44 2004): 481–96, especially 484–88.

[5] This journal entry is the closest we have to a précis of Kierkegaard's political and moral psychology. It is completely coherent with his critique of aestheticism, his several elaborations of the ethical life, his view of Christianity, and his critique of Christendom.

It is important to note that Kierkegaard does not name a single event, person, or party as the cause of the subversion of subjectivity or politics. Rather the disintegration is related to the emergence of a new category that he calls "the numerical," which has many manifestations but is rooted in the communicative modes of modernity, the press bearing a primary responsibility. Perhaps this is best shown by an appeal to a bit of history.

As the press laws of the absolute monarchy lost their bite during the 1840s, the press became the primary medium through which the public's interests could be debated, at least in some small degree, on its own terms. The government, the church, the remnants of the landed nobility, and the rising groups, for instance, the capitalist class, were elitist, closed, hierarchical, and authoritarian. Their pronouncements reflected their own interests, and their policies were to some considerable extent mutually supportive. The press came to reflect the interest of its owners and sponsors, whether they were "liberal," "conservative," focused on a regional interest, or some religious party. Thus the press was ideologically anything but monolithic. By contrast, there was one feature that reduced the press to a single economic and sociological model: the press was commercially competitive, and success depended upon circulation—the numerical (JP, 5:6007). Based on the representation of specialized interests and its dependence upon income based upon circulation, it was indeed only to a very small degree that the public interest could be served by the press. But ironically, the primary beneficiary of all this hubbub was not just the owners of the newspapers, but the growth of political discussion and democracy. Even more ironically, the indicator of the party that exercises real power is the number at the bottom of the balance sheet, the numerical in the most literal sense. Not only is the profit revealed there, but perhaps more important is whether the "the numerical," considered as economic value, has become the most important standard of value in the society.

The emergence of voting as a means of political decision is correlative with the appearance of the modern press as a means of public communication. Both are manifestations of the numerical. Kierkegaard recognizes these as simple facts and as important parameters within which he must exercise his vocation as a Christian writer. But the issue of communicating the claims of God in Christendom becomes problematic. After all, there is an official institution that is charged with supervising, maintaining, and communicating the official religion. Application of the new concept may just open new insights into the operations and ideology of the church.

Kierkegaard initiated his (in)famous "attack on Christendom," because Christendom failed to enunciate Christianity as heterogeneous to the ends and goals of human societies and states. The attack was not just an attack on the church and its hierarchy but was literally against Christendom, considered as an interlaced system of legal, political, and sociological licenses and empowerment for the insiders, the elite classes; and by contrast, oppression, control, and management if not domination for those outside the hierarchical systems. During the revolutionary period of 1848–1849, Bishop J. P. Mynster negotiated some improvements in the tax structure that supported the church, a political achievement of no mean proportions. Mynster's successor, Hans Lassen Martensen, in his funeral oration had characterized Mynster as a man whose memory leads us back "to the whole succession of truth-witnesses that like a holy chain stretches from the days of the Apostles to our own day" (TM, 359), Typically, Kierkegaard did not raise questions about the political and financial matters, but picked up on the use of a religiously vital word "witness."

Kierkegaard's criticism of the use of "witness" to describe Bishop Mynster goes to the very heart of his later view of the Christian life and discipleship. Mynster was a bishop whose livelihood was guaranteed by the taxing power of the state. In turn, the king received the services of the most powerful institution in the country and the widest network of paid professionals to offer their moral influence to support the state in principle and to pray for the king every Sunday, regardless of the wisdom or stupidity of the ends and policies of the state. Mynster had overseen the transition from the absolute monarchy to the constitutional monarchy, transferred the support of the church from the first to the second without a publicly recorded twinge, and endorsed the very politics that engulf it and doom the institution to subservience to the state to this very day. The new insiders who moved in to govern after framing the liberal constitution and overseeing its acceptance managed to accommodate an arrangement with the church hierarchy. Whether a witness or not, Mynster was an astute politician.[6]

For Kierkegaard by contrast, a witness is a life dedicated and at risk. He writes:

---

[6] The authoritative treatment in English of Kierkegaard's struggle against the "People's Church" in English is still Bruce H. Kirmmse's *Kierkegaard in Golden Age Denmark* (Bloomington: Indiana University Press, 1990) 449–81. In this connection, see also Jørgen Bukdahl's *Søren Kierkegaard and the Common Man*, trans. Bruce H. Kirmmse (Grand Rapids: William B. Eerdmans Publishing Company, 2001) 154.

> That one has faith can be demonstrated in only one way: by being willing to suffer for one's faith; and the degree of faith is demonstrated only by the degree of one's willingness to suffer for one's faith.
>
> That is the way Christianity came into the world; served by witnesses who were willing unconditionally to suffer everything for their faith, and actually did come to suffer, to sacrifice life and blood for the faith. (TM, 324)

Accepting the Christian view of the history of Western societies, Kierkegaard wrote in a book published posthumously:

> No, never has any doctrine—served by that which weighs it down and makes it finite by status people and salaried officials—transformed the face of the world… No but Christianity—and this is the crucial point that makes this doctrine other than a doctrine—was served by *witnesses to the truth*, who, instead of having profit and every profit from this doctrine, sacrificed and sacrificed everything for this doctrine, *witnesses to the truth*, who did not, and together with a family, live off the doctrine but lived and died for the doctrine. Because of that, Christianity became power, power, became the power that was able to transform the world. (JFY, 129)

Bishop Hans L. Martensen, Mynster's successor, offered only one counter statement to Kierkegaard's published criticism, now popularly known as the "the attack on Christendom," and after that only silence greeted the latter's continued criticism. What was needed was a dialogue, a public disagreement so that the issues could be brought into the open. There were a few other replies to Kierkegaard's criticism, but no engagement with the primate and power of the church.

The refusal of the People's Church, a political creature if ever there was one, to enter into political discussion was "contemptible," as Kierkegaard said, for the refusal was a denial of its political basis. Against the elitism of Christendom he urged egalitarianism; against the closed, still-authoritarian society he urged public debate; against hierarchy he urged broad participation in the political process by all classes, though he appealed especially to the common humanity of all that had been governed by its "betters" from time immemorial. At the same time, because the newly emerging state, founded on universal male suffrage, had to a considerable degree established private interest as a means to the public good (as a modern liberal state should), Kierkegaard saw the flaws of the new regime from the beginning to be a reissue of some of the flaws of the old regime: aestheticism, hedonism, greed, ambition, the lust to dominate, to name a few of the less endearing of characteristics of human relations. The new liberal state with its official religion was the reincarnation of the old absolutist state and its official religion. The changing of the guard was no more than that. Kierkegaard was one of the first to perceive this deception, and this perception made the attack on Christendom inevitable. That which the new powers guarded remained very much the same: elitism, official piety, hierarchy (based now on market capitalism), and domination of the "have-nots" by the "haves," or as they were recently called, "my base."

This paper has not laid out the legal or the constitutional nature of a Kierkegaardian politics. We have, however, interrogated political reflection using a few of Kierkegaard's categories. Some are critical: the numerical and the political itself; and some positive: the single individual and communication, which assume his philosophical (Socratic) and theological (Judeo-Christian) egalitarianism, and his claims for human equality and human likeness. Positively and negatively, these distinctions point toward a Kierkegaardian politics that can be worked out in the common life. Working toward those goals is at least one way persons who would live as followers of the Christian way and those who follow some other way can give humane political content to their lives.

Key to the sigla of Kierkegaard's works referenced
All volumes are edited and translated by Howard V. Hong and Edna H. Hong. (Princeton: Princeton University Press).

PV *The Point of View*
JP *Journals and Papers*
CUP *Concluding Unscientific Postscript*
TM *The Moment* (previously, *Attack upon Christendom*)
JFY *Judge for Yourselves!*

The Future of Baptist Higher Education[1]

R. KIRBY GODSEY

The future of Baptist higher education has rarely been more fragile. The distrust between Baptist institutions and their denominational constituencies has rarely been more intense. Some Baptist leaders, increasingly under the spell of fundamentalist forces, are becoming systematically more prescriptive regarding the conditions of "fellowship" between the church and the school. And Baptist colleges, one after another, are literally being forced to sacrifice their intellectual integrity in order to assure the flow of funds that is necessary to keep the lights on. Many college administrators find themselves pandering to the religious right, while being afraid, at every moment, that some denominational leader will discover that there is a gay student on campus, or God forbid, a gay faculty member.

In short, Baptist politics are wreaking havoc on the future of Baptist higher education. In state after state, where so many Baptist colleges struggle to make ends meet, the ruling class of Baptists have become increasingly closed, myopic, and disdainful of open inquiry.

So, it is indeed time to ask ourselves about the future of our Baptist institutions in this twenty-first century. If we are to chart a course that offers some hope for the future, we must be

---

[1] Delivered at the Whitsitt Society meeting in Atlanta, Georgia, in June 2006.

prepared to look honestly, with great candor, at our present situation.

Let me begin by observing that I am convinced that Baptists and higher education can chart a course in which they are not alien to one another. The lives of students and the work of Baptists have been profoundly enriched by our common labors. But our present course is perilous. Unless we find the courage to create a relationship based upon mutual respect, Baptists and Baptist churches will come to be regarded as an irrelevant voice in the future of higher education and Baptist educators will have to choose between being Baptist and being educators.

The fraying and the fracturing of relationships between schools and their respective state conventions has become rampant. Lawsuits are erupting in Missouri and Georgia and perhaps Tennessee. Tensions are high. Fear is prevalent. In my own state, Georgia, the Georgia Baptist Convention (GBC) engaged in a protracted lawsuit to retain control of Shorter College. Losing in the state's superior court, the Convention appealed the ruling, and it was finally resolved in Georgia's Supreme Court in a 4-3 ruling. The ruling returned Shorter College to the control of the Georgia Baptist Convention. While still in the glow of that victory, the same Convention took action that ultimately led to the dissolution of the ties between Mercer University and the GBC. Mercer's charter provided for the academic independence of the university, an independence that perennially left the Convention unsatisfied with its inability to exercise full control over the trustee selection or the academic priorities of the university. The flashpoint for the final disintegration of that relationship was the university's commitment to being a "community of respect" that included respect for persons regardless of their sexual orientation. So, the GBC fought vigorously and successfully to regain control of one college and disassociated with another because it could not gain control.

The flashpoints will differ in each institutional setting, but the principles present in every setting revolve around issues of control and the expectations and demands that spring from the financial support provided by conventions.

Financial support is being used to enforce a rigid orthodoxy. If educators are to fulfill their calling to serve God in the unfettered search for truth, colleges and universities cannot become the handmaiden to denominational prescriptions. The university's highest obligation is first and foremost to pursue the truth and to teach the truth to all who come within its boundaries. Contrary to some ardent denominational voices, the commitment to open inquiry and to the open search for truth does not stop at the covers of the Bible. We need never fear the search for truth and any effort to restrict a college's devotion to intellectual freedom and to open inquiry should be unequivocally rejected. Being Baptist should never mean compromising the bedrock educational values which lie at the essence of being a university. An institution cannot be a good Baptist college or university without, first of all, being a good college or university.

A word of caution. If Baptist higher education is to be sustained as a respected force in higher education, we must first be willing to define how we can maintain our Baptist identity with integrity, and second, we must be prepared to work with Baptist constituents to define new paradigms for preserving the relationship between Baptists and higher education.

The first order of business that will be necessary to secure the future of Baptist higher education, is that colleges and universities must themselves be willing to turn inward in order to determine, in their own place and circumstance, what it means, in substance, to be a Baptist university or a Baptist college. Is being Baptist more than about money and history? Setting aside money and the denominational obligations that flow from it, the issue is to identify and define how, if at all, being Baptist shapes the educational agenda of the college or university. What does the college do differently or what priorities are more compelling because it is Baptist? Are we willing, as Baptist educators, to offer a serious alternative to the prevailing forces of secularism in higher education? Perhaps our Baptist identity affects the students who are admitted to be educated. Perhaps it affects how an institution defines a well-educated graduate of the institution. If the university does not or cannot define, in its own setting, apart from external religious pressures, what it means to be Baptist, then the institution should acknowledge that being Baptist relates mostly to their history or to their current receipt of critical financial support. In these cases, being Baptist is hardly about an educational agenda or some defining values. In the twenty-first century, however, relationships based chiefly on funding will become increasingly fragile and a historic relationship that is not translated into living educational priorities will, in my judgment, become a mere footnote to the institutions' endeavors.

I am suggesting that, in the final analysis, the future of Baptist higher education will not depend simply on forces within the state conventions. The inner question is whether we can regain and sustain a sense of vocation about our work as Baptist institutions. The money has dulled our sensibilities. In the rush to secure financial support, we have often eclipsed or ignored the traditions and principles that enable us to make a distinctive contribution to the arena of higher education.

Without coming to terms with our inner sense of destiny, we have no place to stand to discuss our relationship with our Baptist constituents.

After examining our own reason for being and defining what "Baptistness" means to the soul of our institutions, we can then pose the question, "How can we build a relationship with our Baptist constituents that enriches the life of Baptist churches and contributes to the substance and character of our colleges and universities?"

I offer five brief recommendations as a place to begin:

1. First, rethink the selection of trustees. The process for selecting trustees inevitably sets the course for the relationship between denominational bodies and institutions of higher education. The unseemly intrusions of the religious right into the affairs of colleges and universities reflects the fear of a decaying denomination. As a result of these intrusions, major institutions have abandoned their respective Convention relationships in order to maintain their educational integrity.

We have to create new paradigms for selecting the governing boards of Baptist institutions. Boards of trustees should not become watchdogs for theological or political correctness. The practice of denominational bodies exercising exclusive control over the selection of trustees is outmoded and ineffective and it works against the capacity to build genuine partnerships to advance Christian education.

Trustees should not be placed in a setting where they must choose between what is right, or good, or appropriate for the institution and what is acceptable to a denominational constituency. Countless mechanisms can be established whereby church constituencies can be participating partners in the selection of trustees, but church constituents should, in my view, get out of the business of being the exclusive voice in selecting and disciplining boards.

2. Second, elevate mission above politics. The future of Baptist higher education will require that boards of trustees should be accountable, not to a church constituency, but to an institution's mission. It is a tragic mistake to assume that a college or university is not being faithful to its originating church constituency unless its allegiance to that constituency's prevailing doctrines is uncompromising. Achieving accountability in this manner is dead wrong. Church and denominational constituencies are misappropriating their influence by seeking to exercise such control. For schools, the notion of sacrificing educational autonomy for the sake of receiving denominational approval or funding is a treacherous and immoral bargain.

3. Third, replace the language of control. The language of control must yield to the language of cooperation. The rich history of Baptist higher education has been rooted in cooperation, not control, in mutual respect, not coercion.

The history of Baptists is the history of tolerance and freedom. Baptists should not seek to control a Baptist university any more than the university should seek to control the church. Baptist churches must be free. Baptist colleges and universities must be free. Any efforts on the part of the denomination to control the educational program of a Baptist institution are no more acceptable than would be attempts by a Baptist university to control the pulpit. Baptists are free people and free believers. Let the preachers preach; let the teachers teach. God's truth will prevail. Common history, common traditions, and common values, not a received set of doctrines, should bind together the university and the church. We must get beyond the language of control and embrace the language of cooperation.

4. Reclaim the power of administrative courage and leadership. The future of Baptist higher education depends, in part, upon fostering a breed of senior administrators who understand their critical role in the future of Baptist higher education. The leaders of Baptist schools must lead with strength and uncompromising resolve. It is not, after all, the faculty's role to create a climate of open inquiry. The job of faculty is to conduct inquiries openly and to teach and to do research unintimidated by voices that want teaching and research to occur in the service of protecting somebody's "sound doctrine." Making doctrine a boundary for teaching and research leads, inevitably, to a descending spiral of academic decay.

On more than one occasion, I have been confronted by a Georgia pastor bent on culling out the heretics in the Christianity department. They have come determined to conduct an investigation into what was being taught in class or published by the university press. My reply was always the same: "You can come to my office and talk about anything, heretical or otherwise, that you believe occurs at Mercer. But when you leave my office, you have spoken to the last person you can speak to at Mercer."

While boards and faculties have a role to play in assuring academic freedom, the real and practical burden rests squarely with senior administrators who have the will to govern their institutions without caving in to denominational power plays. The future of Baptist higher education, more than ever before, will require administrators who lead with conviction and courage and who understand that the search for truth cannot be sacrificed on the make-believe altar of religious correctness.

5. Finally, Baptist colleges and universities must be willing to invest themselves in helping to preserve the Baptist idea. Historic Baptist principles have been seriously eroded in recent years within the corporate power structures of Baptists. Against all odds, the role of a Baptist university is, in part, to keep alive the light of freedom, kindling the debate among Baptists of differing persuasions and assuring that the fragile freedoms around which Baptists have coalesced are not lost to the dustbin of obsolescence.

The truth is that Baptist institutions of higher education should take greater responsibility for sustaining the substance and the significance of the Baptist witness. As educators, we have grown far too timid and we have been too inattentive to our Baptist heritage. Preserving the Baptist witness cannot be done by the church alone. In a world that is being sharply divided by the conflicting and misguided values of both secularism and fundamentalism, our Baptist colleges and universities should embody a better way—a way that holds high the power of the Baptist idea of freedom and faithfulness. It is possible to believe and to think. Our high calling is to engage in the disciplined pursuit of knowledge, while making clear that knowledge alone will not be enough. The calling of Baptist higher education is not only to challenge the mind, but to nurture the human spirit, and to be devoted to both freedom and faith.

It is not at all clear whether colleges and universities can maintain constructive partnerships with their historic church constituents. But I believe that, if it is possible, both the church and the school must learn to affirm one another and support each other without doctrinal encumbrances or political conditions. If Baptist colleges and universities are to be sustained in the twenty-first century, we must redefine the structure and character of how the church and the schools relate. Money and doctrine cannot be our solitary or even primary connection. Baptist schools have to come to grips with whether their devotion to being Baptist is only "skin" deep. That is, if Baptist churches or state conventions have less "skin" in the game, will the school's commitment to being Baptist diminish? If so, being Baptist is, candidly, inauthentic. Churches have to determine if they are willing to support higher education without seeking to control the academic agenda. If not, their commitment to education is disingenuous.

The high calling of Baptist colleges or universities in the twenty-first century is to be an independent, courageous, and compassionate interpreters among Baptists who, we should remember, are a pluralistic people. While the university should always remain open to the criticism and counsel of Baptists and Baptist congregations, the university should also remind the church that trading freedom for certainty is a precarious bargain.

Baptist institutions should be cauldrons of "straight talk" in a world where religious demagoguery is wholesaling bad religion and undermining the integrity of the Christian witness. So, let mutual respect and mutual criticism prevail. Colleges and universities will be strengthened by the criticism and the nurturing support of the church. Even so, the role of colleges and universities is not to be obedient to the denomination. Their role is to educate and nurture the young, who, after all, embody the future of our congregations. These young are the very hope of Baptist life in this new century. God help us to find the wisdom and the courage to find our way through the shadows of distrust and coercive control. If the light dawns, the church and the school will become enormous sources of energy and hope for one another.

What Has Happened to Baptists and the First Amendment?[1]

WALTER B. SHURDEN

The text for this specific conference and for the entire First Freedoms Project is the First Amendment to the Constitution of the United States. Ratified as the law of the land on 15 December 1791, the First Amendment goes like this: "Congress shall make no law respecting an establishment of religion, or prohibiting the free exercise thereof; or abridging the freedom of speech, or of the press: or the right of the people peaceably to assemble, and to petition the Government for a redress of grievances." Those forty-five words contain a radical commitment to five freedoms for an open society: freedom of religion, freedom of speech, freedom of the press, freedom to assemble, and freedom to petition the government.

---

[1] I delivered this address at the First Freedoms Project Conference sponsored by Associated Baptist Press, Baptist Joint Committee, and *Baptists Today* at the First Baptist Church in Washington, DC, on 14 April 2005. The First Freedoms Project is an effort by these three organizations to underscore the importance of the freedoms spelled out in the First Amendment to the Constitution of the United States. Heretofore unpublished, I now revise and dedicate this essay to Edd Rowell. Edd is a student of many things, among them is the historic role of Baptists in American life. He has edited numerous books on Baptist history and Baptist theology, including several of my books published by Mercer University Press. While celebrating the contribution of Baptists to religious liberty and the separation of church and state in American culture, Edd Rowell is also a gentle critic of his faith family when he sees them deviating from their traditional emphases.

So, why should a group of Baptists, of all religious denominations in America, sponsor a First Freedoms Project, anyway? Because, if Brent Walker[2] is even in the ballpark—if Brent Walker is even in the *neighborhood* of the ballpark!—in his jarring assessment that the First Amendment would not pass if put for vote to the American public today, the spirit of the First Amendment is neck-deep in trouble.

A recent study bears out Brent Walker's terribly dark assessment. A survey of 100,000 high school students in America concluded that one out of three students believes that the First Amendment goes *too far* in the rights it guarantees![3] That last sentence ought to be absolutely horrendous to your ears. In fact, that sentence reminds me of a phone call we got about 12:30 one night when we were living in Louisville, Kentucky. The call was from Wayne Dehoney, pastor of Walnut Street Baptist Church in the city. He said, "Walter, this is Wayne Dehoney, I just received a call from Cullman, Alabama, and Grady Nutt was killed in a plane crash tonight. I knew that you were close friends, so I am calling to tell you." I remember saying in stunned shock and disbelief, "Wayne, you are going to have to say that again." As a good pastor, he said, "I understand." And then he said slowly once more, "I received a call from Cullman, Alabama, and Grady Nutt was killed in an airplane crash tonight."

---

[2] J. Brent Walker is the executive director of the Baptist Joint Committee for Religious Liberty in Washington, DC, and he is one of the leading advocates for religious freedom and separation of church and state in America.

[3] See "The Future of the First Amendment: What America's High School Students Think about Their Freedoms" posted on 12 April 2005 at http://www.mindfully.org/Reform/2005/Future-First-Amendment31jan05.htm.

If you hear it carefully, the sentence about the high school students and the First Amendment has all the tone and sound of a death announcement about someone you love. So I want to repeat it, slowly, so that it will sink in: one in three high school students in this republic says that the First Amendment of the Constitution of the United States goes too far in the rights it guarantees to you as a citizen!

The survey did not end there, however. It contained more surprises. For example, nearly three-fourths say either they don't know how they feel about the First Amendment or they take it for granted. More shocking still, only one-half of the students surveyed said that a newspaper should be allowed to publish freely without government approval of stories.

My friends, we are talking about my grandchildren's future here! This is America's tomorrow speaking! One-third of them want the freedoms of the First Amendment curbed. And one-half of them want newspapers to secure government approval for their stories!! These are astonishing and inconceivable attitudes for high school students in the United States of America. This survey is a terrible, scary phone call in the middle of the night about what has happened in our nation.

And the situation differs little among many in our Baptist denomination. And this, also, is a major reason for the First Freedoms Project. I am sixty-eight years old. I have been in the ministry since I was eighteen years old. The math is easy. Eighteen from sixty-eight is fifty. For a full half century now, I have been roaming the Baptist yard, mostly in the white Baptist yard of the South to be sure, loving and being loved by Baptist people, observing Baptist practices and preaching, celebrating with them the principles for which they have stood, and studying, teaching, writing, and preaching our Baptist heritage.

And here's the truth: when I entered the Baptist ministry as a youngster in 1955, and for at least thirty years afterward, if you preached a sermon in a Baptist church on the separation of church and state and religious liberty or freedom of conscience, you would have them snoring in their pews in a matter of minutes! The Benediction became wake-up time. All of that "freedom stuff" enshrined in the First Amendment was old hat to Baptist folk back then.

But not today! Today you preach a sermon on absolute religious liberty for all people, on genuine separation of church and state, on freedom of conscience and freedom of the press, and you will begin to feel "sanctuary electricity." "Sanctuary electricity" is when the preacher viscerally knows that the right button has just been hit. Negative energy begins to flow in the room, and it showers the pulpit.

To the contrary,

if you preach a sermon in many Baptist churches today and say, so as to reinforce their prejudices, that the phrase "separation of church and state" is not in the Constitution, and

if you preach that the First Amendment has been misinterpreted and taken too far, and

if you preach that certain religious groups in this country need to conform to our particular religious customs, and

if you preach that our nation is going to hell in a hand basket because of a judiciary that does not acknowledge our particular theological values and symbols and,

if you preach a distorted historical interpretation that this country has always been a Christian nation but is now losing it moorings,...

if that's what you tell them at 11:00 on Sunday morning, sanctuary electricity will become sanctuary applause.

So what has happened to Baptists regarding the First Amendment?

Among other things, we Baptists have distinguished ourselves by neglect of our own heritage. The understanding of Baptist history for many Baptists goes all the way back to the last resolution adopted at the last meeting of their particular Baptist convention. Candidly, we are a historically illiterate people. Unanchored, we float with the prevailing political and religious culture. And we float, unanchored, because we do not know the Baptist story.

Except for a small minority, our Baptist people simply do not know our heritage. And while it may be a waste of time, we must plead and beg in the First Freedoms Project for the Baptist people to take some time simply to read our stories. For example, few Baptists know the story of Dr. John Clarke of Rhode Island, a physician who worked on the soul of a sick society as well as the bodies of sick people.

Who was John Clarke? Well, put it this way: if Billy Graham was the most influential Baptist in twentieth-century America, John Clarke was the single most influential Baptist of seventeenth-century America. He was just that big in our denominational story.

In 1652, John Clarke wrote the single most important Baptist book of seventeenth-century America. It was one of the earliest Baptist classics. He called it *Ill Newes from New England*. *Ill Newes* [4] was a seventeenth-century bugle blast for a radical religious freedom that would scare the daylights out of some

---

[4] For a copy of Clarke's classic, see *Colonial Baptists: Massachusetts and Rhode Island* (New York: Arno Press, 1980). For information email aycrpug@yahoo.com or go to www.ayerpub.com. The mailing address is 1 Lower Mill Rd.; North Stratford NH 03590.

Baptists today. It was a fervent call for the First Amendment 140 years before the First Amendment.

Why did Clarke write it? He wrote it because he and two other men violated the laws of Massachusetts by attempting to hold a Baptist worship service at a blind preacher's house in the town of Lynn. They were arrested, sent to a Boston prison, and one of his friends, Obadiah Holmes, was whipped on the streets of Boston. Clarke, writing from prison, pled for the Puritan establishment to afford him free speech. He asked them to debate him on the issues of separation of church and state and liberty of conscience. When they refused, he promptly wrote *Ill Newes from New England* and sent it to the Parliament of Old England. He was trying to marshal all the powers of Old England against the abuses of conscience in New England.

Ill Newes is important for Baptists in contemporary America for many reasons. Read *Ill Newes* carefully, and then read some of the legislation proposed in this city and in state capitols around this country today and you may want to write a sequel to John Clarke's work. You could call it *Ill Newes from Twenty-First Century America*.

With age, we Baptists have developed cataracts. Our denominational vision, once crystal clear on First Amendment issues, today is opaque. Impervious to the light of our denominational history and family commitments, we have blocked out heroic chapters of our very own story. I discovered that our word "cataract" comes from a Greek word *kataraktes* that comes from two other words, one of which means "down" and the other means "to fall" or "headlong." These denominational cataracts that have accompanied our Baptist aging have caused us as a people to fall headlong down from the vision of freedom that once possessed us and that we proudly owned. We no longer see clearly on First Amendment issues, because we have lost our theological vision that God built freedom into the fabric of the universe.

Part of the reason for the cloudy vision is that today the issues appear in more civil, more subtle, and more ambiguous ways. Just listen to the language: "faith-based charity." "Faith"? What's to oppose there? "Charity" Who can be against that? "Prayer in public schools." Well, what is prayer going to hurt? Why not? "The posting of the ten commandments!" Where's the harm in that? "Vouchers for taxpayers." Is that not the fair thing? "What's the big deal with these harmless efforts?" ordinary Baptists ask. The big deal is that these represent *Ill Newes from Twenty-First Century America*. And they represent *Ill Newes* for both religion and government.

We now have Baptist politicians who get elected to public office by minimizing the separation of church and state and maximizing the claim that this is a Christian nation. When they do want to demonstrate their commitment to a belief in First Amendment pluralism, they refer to this republic, expansively in their minds, as a Judeo-Christian nation, forgetting all other devout religionists and those with no religion at all. "If they don't like America the way it is, let them leave," is the way I heard it from one Baptist layperson, which may have been the exact sentiment of the Native Americans who saw us stepping on shore. It was precisely the sentiment that the Puritans and Anglicans had toward Baptists in the seventeenth and eighteenth centuries.

My hope for the First Freedoms Project is that it will reclaim the Baptist people for the Baptist heritage, that it will cause us to rededicate ourselves to the conviction that *freedom* goes to the very heart of our theology and identity. *Freedom* is at the heart of our denominational DNA.

The Baptist affirmation of freedom is not simply an American ideal that we happened to embrace. For us, freedom is spiritual before it is political; it is theological before it is cultural; it was a part of the Baptist Enlightenment before there was an Age of Enlightenment.

Quite simply, freedom of conscience is the will of God for the Baptist heritage. Long before freedom of conscience was central to being an American citizen, it was at the core of what it meant to be Baptist.

I hope the First Freedoms Project will act as a catalyst on our churches, a catalyst that will cause them to tell our denominational story. And it is a denominational story marinated in the love of freedom and preceding the First Amendment.

A number of other things have happened to Baptists and the First Amendment. We have, for example, run upon some competition every bit as tough as the seventeenth-century Puritans and eighteenth-century Anglicans. We have run upon a stubborn secularism and also upon a baffling pluralism. Each engenders fear. And fear is the dominant emotion of our time. Fear goes a long way in explaining the timidity regarding the five freedoms of the First Amendment. When people really find out what the First Amendment says, like those high school students, their desire for security outruns their thirst for freedom.

Just a very brief word about secularism. Secularism frightens many of the religious among us. And, quite frankly, no devout person of faith, regardless of the religious tradition, can be without some sympathies for that sentiment. Secularism is as much a worldview as any religion. It frightens. Many religious Americans, or so it seems to me, are fearful of the very same thing that some Muslims in the East are fearful of: a pervasive secularism that not only changes the religious environment but abolishes it. I understand that. It is ironic, however, that some of the same Americans who desperately want Iraq and Iran to establish secular republics want the Congress of the United States to legislate a "Judeo-Christian Nation." And Baptists of that persuasion need some old-fashioned, aisle-walking, altar-bumping, heart-rending rededication to the passions and principles of our ancestors, especially as those principles touch on the First Amendment. Historically, Baptists have been willing to take on secularism in the free market of ideas. And they have done it with confidence. They have done it with success. And they have done it without the aid and assistance of government.

Moreover, we Baptists, like all religious Americans, have also had to confront in the last forty or fifty years a growing and baffling religious pluralism in this country. The floodgates of religious diversity opened in 1965 with the Immigration and Naturalization Act. And so we now have, as Diana Eck said in the title of her important 2001 book, *A New Religious America*,[5] a religious America more diverse than our ancestors could ever have imagined.

Look at what's happened to us. During the colonial period we Protestants, except for Native Americans, had about the only game in the land. Protestants, therefore, feared Protestants. Religious prejudice ensued. Then came the Irish and Italian Catholics with their rosaries and names ending in "a" and "i." Now Protestants feared Catholics. Religious prejudice ensued. But while some Protestants refused to acknowledge Catholicism as a bona fide expression of the

---

[5] Diana L. Eck, *A New Religious America: How a "Christian Country" Has Become the World's Most Religiously Diverse Nation* (New York: Harper Collins, 2001).

Christian faith, the Catholic masses simply could not be ignored. So Christians, both Protestants and Catholics, combined to form a shaky religious alliance, and, retained, for some people at least, the language that America was a "Christian" nation. Then the Jews, the Christians' cousins, came ashore. Now Protestants and Catholics feared Jews. Religious prejudice ensued. Eventually, we found new language. We were now a "Judeo-Christian nation."

But today, we confront names that we cannot pronounce and religious traditions about which we know next to nothing. So how do we self-describe religious America today? Listen to our language and you will discern our prejudices. Listen to our language and you will understand the limitations we place on the First Amendment.

I believe that Dr. Jonathan Sacks, the Chief Rabbi of the United Hebrew Congregations of the Commonwealth, is correct when he says that "globalization is summoning the world's great faiths to a supreme challenge." And that supreme challenge comes in the form of a question: "Can we recognize God's image in one who is not in my image?"[6] That question, precisely because of the First Amendment, will become more relevant in America than any country in the world.

What do Baptists, that small and noisy band of only one segment of only one of the world's great religions, bring to the table of interfaith dialogue? Do we Baptists have anything at all of value to say? I think so, and I believe that Baptist theologian Charles Kimball said much of it back in 2002 in his deservedly popular book, *When Religion Becomes Evil.*[7]

---

[6] Jonathan Sacks, *The Dignity of Difference: How to Avoid the Clash of Civilizations*, rev. ed. (London/New York: Continuum, 2003) 17.

[7] Charles L. Kimball, *When Religion Becomes Evil* (San Francisco: HarperCollins Publishers, 2002).

I always thought it instructive to turn Kimball's title on its head and to read his book from the point of view of *When Religion Becomes Healthy*. For while Kimball described some "evil" characteristics of religion in his book, he also inevitably sketched the outline of "good," "positive," and "healthy" religion. In his closing chapter he said, "As we have explored each of the warning signs of corrupted religion, we have seen how correctives were always present within each tradition. Our study of the pathological has helped to elucidate the healthy" (187). I fear this healthy dimension of religion in Kimball's book was overlooked. What *does* religion look like when it becomes healthy? Listen for echoes of the First Amendment as I serve up quotations from Kimball.

1. Kimball said, "Freedom *of* religion is a good thing. So is freedom *from* the religion others may wish to impose on those who differ" (25). Healthy religion is religion free from coercion. And there is the Baptist tradition!

2. Kimball said, "The uncritical mixing of religious, political, military, and economic realms in the missionary conquests...contradicts the cherished principle of the separation of church and state" (63). Healthy religion advocates some separation between religion and government. And there is the Baptist tradition!

3. Kimball said, "...blind obedience is a sure sign of corrupt religion. Beware of any religious movement that seeks to limit the intellectual freedom and individual integrity of its adherents. When individual believers abdicate personal responsibility and yield to the authority of a charismatic leader or become enslaved to particular ideas or teachings, religion can easily become the framework for violence and destruction" (72). Healthy religion protects and affirms the conscience of the individual. And there is the Baptist tradition!

4. Kimball said of the religious sect that released deadly nerve gas in sixteen Tokyo subway stations in 1995, that it "provided little room for independent opinions or debate among adherents" (82). Healthy religion provides not only for independent opinions but for "debate among adherents." And there is the Baptist tradition!

Do you understand why I once told Charles Kimball that I thought he was unaware of how Baptist a book he had written? We Baptists, though often perceived as excessively sectarian and fundamentalist, bring a wealth of ideas to the world of religious pluralism. And the freedom that we bring to the table does not cancel the faith we tenaciously hold.

What can Baptists do today about the first amendment?

When William Carey wrote his famous essay that catapulted Baptists into the arena of world missions, he had three "p's" that Baptists had to heed. Carey said that Baptists had to plan, to pray, and to pay in order to form a world mission enterprise. We must do at least that much—plan, pray, and pay—to support the First Freedoms Project and the First Amendment to the Constitution of the United States. But let me try to be a bit more specific.

First, we can and we must teach our Baptist stories. Baptists can find salvation from fear in our own stories, stories of John Clarke and Roger Williams and Thomas Gould and William Screven and Isaac Backus and John Leland. And I am convinced that we must find some way to teach those stories to the forty-and-younger age group. The place to start is not in adult seminars on Sunday evenings where the only ones present are those who grew up on Baptist Training Union and already believe what we are saying. The place to start is in vacation Bible schools and youth Sunday schools. We need curriculum materials for our young people, and I am glad to say that some progress is being made here. We need more, however. We need a vacation Bible school curriculum called "The First Freedoms Project." Is there a publisher in the sound of my voice?

Second, we can and we must support school boards that work to uphold the First Amendment in the face of enormous pressures. Why, we could even start a campaign to post the Ten Amendments, the Bill of Rights, in the schoolhouses and courthouses of this country. And then we could support a corresponding campaign to post the Ten Commandments in the church houses and the synagogues of the land where they rightfully belong.

Third, Carey was right. We must ante up. We must dig deep to support those good organizations such as the Baptist Joint Committee, *Baptists Today*, and the Associated Baptist Press who are seeking to educate our churches and our citizens. Bruce Prescott gave good advice when he said that a good rule of thumb for conscientious stewardship is that if the people asking for your money do not support liberty of conscience then they don't deserve your money. Some historically informed Baptists need to "park" some of God's money at the doorsteps of the First Freedoms Project. Do you have some of that money?

Four, we can read and stay informed. Have you noticed that each of the three organizations sponsoring the First Freedoms Project is in the information business? They and many others provide more than we can read on issues of religion's relationship to government. Freedom of the press is crucial to them and to us.

Five, and finally, and maybe more important than anything else that can be said, we can approach the task with the passion that it demands. I believe that in the great moral struggles of human history passion wins. Like you, I believe that this is a moral universe and that truth and justice are built-in components of our world. I do not believe, however, that truth and justice always prevail. And I certainly do not believe that truth and justice prevail unassisted. Truth and justice triumph only when passionate people act passionately about issues of truth and justice. The First Amendment is a justice issue.

The Baptist battle cry for religious freedom and separation of church and state eventually prevailed in America because veins in Baptist necks bulged red at the thought of *any* kind of religious discrimination. Truth and justice needed friends. Baptists, along with Quakers, Presbyterians, and some level-headed secularists, befriended truth and justice.

What would happen today if Baptists—fundamentalist Baptists, liberal Baptists, conservative Baptists, and moderate Baptists, black Baptists and white Baptists and ethnic Baptists of all kinds—what would happen if those Baptists acted out of their heritage and recovered the unmitigated passion that characterized our humble ancestors for the First Amendment to the Constitution of the United States? Here is what would happen.

We would demand that the freedom that we passionately won for ourselves be gladly granted to all people, not simply to people like ourselves.

We would demand that Caesar not make an establishment of "the Judeo-Christian tradition" or, worse, of one narrow theological interpretation of the Christian faith.

We would remind our fellow citizens that this really is a democratic republic, not a theocratic state.

We would implore churches to keep their hands out of Caesar's trough for dollars to supplement Christ's ministry.

We would ask churches to look at those countries with established religions and see how long it takes to find a vital and vibrant faith. I believe for a number of reasons that Baptists have been right to insist that religious faith must be voluntary and freely chosen, but one of the major reasons is because voluntarism creates vital churches and vital faith.

Someone asked Helen Keller if anything was worse than losing one's sight. "Yes," she said, "losing one's vision." We Baptists have work to do to keep the vision alive that birthed us, that gave us our very existence, and that gave us a place of respect in American society. We have a magnanimous vision. It is a vision that transcends us. It is no navel-gazing, self-fixated vision, but a vision that includes the freedom of all people. It is a theological vision that intersects and reinforces those forty-five words and five freedoms of the First Amendment.

One way to sin is to go limp, to avoid responsibility, to play dead, to lose our passion for preeminent principles.[8] Being "moderate" will not win the minds of the American people for the First Amendment. For me, one of the saddest lines in all of Holy Scripture comes from the little fellow with the one talent: "I was afraid and I went and hid your talent in the ground."

Fear loses. Passion wins.

---

[8] For an elaboration of this kind of sinning, see Cornelius Plantinga, Jr., *Not the Way It's Supposed to Be: A Breviary of Sin* (Grand Rapids: William B. Eerdmans Publishing Company, 1995) 187. Walter B. Shurden is executive director of the Center for Baptist Studies and Callaway Professor of Christianity at Mercer University in Macon, Georgia.

A Church with Wheels

GRAYDON F. SNYDER

> Wherever the Spirit would go, the creatures went, and the wheels rose along with them; for the Spirit of the living creatures was in the wheels. (Ezek 1:20.)

Since 1930, the hub of the Church of the Brethren, a Free Church denomination, could be located on the West Side of Chicago. Included in the hub was Bethany Hospital, the only Church of the Brethren medical center; Bethany Theological Seminary, the only Church of the Brethren seminary; and in nearby Elgin, Illinois, the denominational headquarters. Consequently, Chicago First Church of the Brethren was one of the largest and most influential congregations in the denomination. Sometime in the 1970s, the Chicago hub lost its wheels. Already in the early 1960s Bethany Theological Seminary had moved to Oak Brook in order to train students in a "less stressful suburban environment." Then in the '70s the community around First Church, and the membership of the church itself, became increasingly African-American. The hospital could not survive on Medicaid payments so eventually it shifted over into the United Church of Christ hospital system, now known as Advocate. The church was severely affected by these changes. Membership (highly dependent on the seminary and hospital) dwindled radically. Then in the late '70s disaster struck. Boiler problems and roofing damage forced the members out of the sanctuary. Subsequently they met on the first floor of the adjacent parish house. There were seventeen members at that time. We remember them as the Faithful Seventeen. Well, with some radical fundraising the church was finally rebuilt. Membership grew once more. But the life of the church depended heavily on these Faithful Seventeen—no, better yet, the women of the Faithful Seventeen. You see First Church had lost its masculine wheels. The hub was gone.

The Faithful Seventeen did exceptionally well, but indeed something was missing: men working together. In 2002 an unanticipated new wheel entered our faith community—a Foard to be precise. David Foard, an African American, had lived in the community many years. He was interested in a church that would help improve the neighborhood. So after a few Sundays, Foard urged the men to do something. It worked. One Saturday the men sold barbecue dinners and raised over $1,000 for college scholarship aid. The men were enthused. They met to celebrate the success and plan another event. Foard insisted there should be an organization. What should be it called? BMW, of course—Brethren Men Working. The wheels were back.

Who Could Drive the BMW?

Our first organization was a bit tentative. Foard was asked to be the primary driver. The secondary driver was Walter Thurmond, a member since the days when Martin Luther King, Jr., used First Church as his office. It seems simple, but it was not. The pastor of First Church, Orlando Redekopp, was also a member of the BMW. Some of our group, raised in strong African-American church communities, assumed the pastor would always be the driver, or, at least, determine who the alternate driver could be. Tradition dies hard. We had a fish fry and yard sale in June 2005. Following the fish fry we had things that needed to be stored. There was considerable discussion about the correct procedure. A talented newcomer from the neighborhood, Jimmy Williams, also African American, asked: Where is the pastor? We must call and ask him what we should do? Answer: He is in Arizona with a Christian Peacemaker Team. Anyway, Jimmy, this is a BMW project. The problem is ours. We will make the decision. We are the drivers.

WHO COULD RIDE IN THE BMW?

That also seems simple. Any man in First Church could ride in the BMW. A far greater problem than who could ride and drive is by what name we address each other in public. Every multicultural church will have to face the name issue. The traditional Brethren are clear: no titles and always first names. So in Brethren parlance Foard is David, Bevly is Charles, Thurman is Walter. It didn't take us long to realize that using first names for these three particular members would appear demeaning. Plantation owners addressed slaves by their first name. First names signified subservience. If Caucasian members of the BMW publicly used David, Charles, and Walter, it would appear to many in the community that whites were making blacks second-class citizens. After much discussion it was decided that the names Mr. Foard, Mr. Bevly, and Mr. Thurman should be used. Despite these advances, the BMW van went into reverse. There are three men in BMW with doctor's degrees. What should they to be called? Most of the African Americans, especially the more recent members, must refer to at least two of these men as doctor. It would be disrespectful before the entire community not to do so. Even the Brethren tradition of equality could not break through these issues of respect, dignity, and appropriateness. It has occurred to all us that the solution lies right before our eyes. Brother. Yes, brother. The appropriate title for all the members of BMW, for all Brethren men! And we do use it frequently. However, "brother" is the address used between African-American men. Dare black and white use it in public? Then there is the African-American term "cuz" (cousin) for very good friends. We can't go there, either. So we men all ride in the BMW, but we are not certain about how we should address each other. Perhaps we can never be certain as long as race is an issue in America.

SAMENESS

The issue facing this local Church of the Brethren in Chicago has an ancient history. The Brethren started in Germany in the early eighteenth century. They followed the Anabaptist rejection of the state church with its ecclesiastical hierarchy attached to a political hierarchy. At the same time contemporary Pietism, found in Halle, influenced them to think of themselves as an ecclesiola in ecclesia, a small group church. As a result the first Brethren, like the Quakers, rejected class and hierarchical distinctions. Titles like doctor, reverend, and sir were forbidden.

The biblical tradition behind this comes from Matthew 23:8–12: "But you are not to be called rabbi, for you have one teacher, and you are all students.[1] And call no one your father on earth, for you have one Father—the one in heaven. Nor are you to be called instructors, for you have one instructor, the Messiah.[2] The greatest among you will be your servant. All

[1] Greek, "brothers."

[2] Greek, "the Christ."

who exalt themselves will be humbled, and all who humble themselves will be exalted."

Jesus strictly forbade distinctions. In fact, he even countered his own presumed hierarchical Rock passage in Matthew 16:8 with a communal understanding of the faith community: "Truly I tell you, whatever you bind on earth will be bound in heaven, and whatever you loose on earth will be loosed in heaven. Again, truly I tell you, if two of you agree on earth about anything you ask, it will be done for you by my Father in heaven. For where two or three are gathered in my name, I am there among them" (18:18–20).

While the first Brethren took seriously the words of Jesus they also believed the words of Paul in Galatians 3:28: "There is no longer Jew or Greek, there is no longer slave or free, there is no longer male and female; for all of you are one in Christ Jesus." Paul believed the dividing walls had been broken down by Jesus (Ephesians 3:14-18), so he spoke of "sameness" or "equality." It was Paul's belief in equality that made him overlook class, ethnic, and sexual differences.[3] Still we can hardly believe that Paul espoused a human *via negative* or apophasis, so to speak. That is, would he actually have created a common humanity, that is sameness by eliminating such differences as race, gender, and social position? Jewish scholar Daniel Boyarin argues that Paul believed in such a sameness because he was "motivated by a Hellenistic desire for the One, which among other things produced an ideal of a universal human essence, beyond difference and hierarchy."[4] The issue of "sameness" is complex as a philosophical

---

[3] Daniel Boyarin, *A Radical Jew: Paul and the Politics of Identity* (Berkeley: University of California Press, 1994) 85.

[4] Ibid., 7, 9, 156.

problem,[5] and well established as well as a genetic theory.[6] Rather than holding to such a comprehensive theory, it may be Paul so radically reduced identity markers that Jews and Gentiles could share in the same faith community without a major conflict.[7] Whatever the case, serious difficulties arose in the Pauline "sameness theology." Earlier in the letter to the Galatians, Paul had written of the sameness dilemma. The famous Antioch meal with Peter and the Jerusalem contingent demonstrates the issue:

> But when Cephas came to Antioch, I opposed him to his face, because he stood self-condemned; for until certain people came from James, he used to eat with the Gentiles. But after they came, he drew back and kept himself separate for fear of the circumcision faction. And the other Jews joined him in this hypocrisy, so that even Barnabas was led astray by their hypocrisy. But when I saw that they were not acting consistently with the truth of the gospel, I said to Cephas before them all, "If you, though a Jew, live like a Gentile and not like a

---

[5] David Wiggins, *Sameness and Substance* (Cambridge: Harvard University Press, 1980). He doubts that difference arises from various historical situations (182)

[6] Current DNA research shows that all modern humans have the same DNA source. See Steve Olson, *Mapping Human History: Discovering the Past through our Genes* (Boston: Houghton Mifflin Company, 2002) 38–39.

[7] John Barclay, "Neither Jew nor Greek: Multiculturalism and the New Perspective on Paul," in Mark G. Brett, *Ethnicity and the Bible* (Leiden: E. J. Brill, 1996) 197–14, see also pp. 212–14.

Jew, how can you compel the Gentiles to live like Jews?" (Gal 2:11–14)

Peter and Barnabas had been the same as the Gentile Christians until the Jerusalem Christians arrived. Then Peter and Barnabas shifted tables. Differentiation overcame sameness. For most readers the distinction between Peter's group over against Paul's group has been seen as a conflict between Jew and Greek. The Jews could not eat with the Greeks because the food was not kosher, or because the Greeks were not circumcised. This much-debated issue need not concern us here. We only note that differentiated identity created conflict in the Antioch house church. It was assumed to be an "inter-" racial conflict.

In recent studies some New Perspective scholars, however, have argued that Paul did not see himself in conflict with Judaism. Instead of an inter-conflict it was an intra-conflict.[8] In contrast to older studies more recent works on Paul deny that Paul is a source of anti-Semitism.[9] The conflict

---

[8] James Dunn, "Echoes of Intra-Jewish Polemic in Paul's Letter to the Galatians," *Journal of Biblical Literature* 112/3 (1993): 459–77.

[9] One of the first to argue for a Paul who considered the Gentile Christians as extension of the Jews was Lloyd Gaston, *No Stone on Another: Studies in the Significance of the Fall of Jerusalem in the Synoptic Gospels* (Leiden: E. J. Brill, 1970). Differentiation only occurred when the fall of Jerusalem was interpreted as the rejection of Israel (e.g., Matthew 23:37–39). See also Gaston's analysis of Paul's critique of Israel in *Paul and the Torah* (Vancover: University of British Columbia Press, 1987),135-150. See John G. Gager, *The Origins of Anti-Semitism: Attitudes toward Judaism in Pagan and*

between the two parties at Antioch arose over differences between Jewish Christians who saw their heritage in Judaism and Greek Christians who also perceived their heritage to be from Judaism in a different way. The problem arose between different types of Jewish Christians, not between Jews and Gentiles. It was "intra." How did Paul solve the issue? He did not suggest or insist that either group change its tradition. Instead he offered them a community formed by "justification by faith" rather than by ancient, powerful traditions that direct corporate life (law): "We ourselves are Jews by birth and not Gentile sinners; yet we know that a person is justified not by the works of the law but through faith in Jesus Christ. And we have come to believe in Christ Jesus, so that we might be justified by faith in Christ, and not by doing the works of the law, because no one will be justified by the works of the law" (Gal 2:15–16).

Some readers of Paul have seen in "justification by faith/grace" a means of divine acceptance that contrasts with works of the law. They may have failed to see justification by faith as a way of overcoming communal differences—a way for

---

Christian Antiquity (Oxford: Oxford University Press, 1985) 197–212, and his *Reinventing Paul* (Oxford: Oxford University Press, 2000). The rejection (of Jews) and replacement (new Israel) had to happen when there were Gentiles that knew nothing of Judasim (pp. 43-75. See also pp. 69 and 75.). Put another way, Terence Donaldson, *Paul and the Gentiles: Remapping of the Apostle's Convictional World* (Minneapolis: Fortress, 1997) believes Paul taught an "intra-" (both/and) community between the time of cross and the time of the parousia. When the parousia did not occur, the Jewish/Christian relationship turned "inter-"" (p. 236).

sameness to occur in the midst of differences.[10] In Galatians, Paul describes a community based on justification by faith rather than inherited traditions: "By contrast, the fruit of the Spirit is love, joy, peace, patience, kindness, generosity, faithfulness, gentleness, and self-control. There is no law against such things. And those who belong to Christ Jesus have crucified the flesh with its passions and desires. If we live by the Spirit, let us also be guided by the Spirit. Let us not become conceited, competing against one another, envying one another" (Gal 5:22–26).

The issue in our Chicago neighborhood was not anti-Semitism or the rejection of our Jewish heritage (though that prejudice lives on in Chicago). Our problem is black-white racial prejudice.[11] We live in a city that consists of many cultures, primarily Caucasian, African-American, and Hispanic. The Caucasians have the power and consistently use it to their advantage over African Americans and Hispanics. First Church of the Brethren exists in a very low income African-American section (East Garfield Park). People know very well the impact of white prejudice.[12] They experience it every day. In Dunn's

---

[10] Barclay, "Neither Jew nor Greek," 213.

[11] A constant sameness problem. For example, South African Robin M. Petersen contrasts racism and even multiracism with non-racism (sameness). See his "Discourses of Difference and Sameness in South Africa: Race, Racism and Non-Racialism," chap. 3 of *Sameness and Difference: Problems and Potentials in South African Civil Society*, ed. James R. Cochrane and Bastienne Klein, South African Philosophical Studies, I, 2000).

[12] Sylvia Hood Washington, *Packing Them In: An Archaeology of Environmental Racism in Chicago, 1865-1954* (Lanham MD: Lexington Books, 2005) 53–54.

terminology, it is definitely an "inter-" situation. East Garfield Park became African American about 1963. At first the congregation at First Church might have shared the "inter-" prejudices, but that has gradually dissipated. The Brethren theology of similarity began to appear in the church, but even the presence of Martin Luther King, with his office in the First Church building, could not stop the "inter-" struggles of Chicago's East Garfield Park.[13]

When the men of First Church got wheels, that is became a church group called BMW, the issue of "intra-" appeared. "Inter-" had disappeared. As with the Galatians, faith became the solution. We learned we could deal with traditional, deeply entrenched traditions, yet become a caring and vibrant group. Faith was the answer. The white Brethren men were practical and calculating. The African-American men trusted God. When we had a barbecue the African-American men said 200 dinners would be sold. God would see to it. The white Brethren said it was impossible. Even if the cause were good, 100 meals would be the maximum. We sold 200 meals. We planned to celebrate Martin Luther King Day on a Sunday. The white Brethren agreed and said to plan for seventy-five present. The African Americans said God would send 150. Somewhat more than 150 attended. The Brethren

---

[13] Taylor Branch, *At Canaan's Edge: America in the King Years, 1965-6* (New York: Simon & Schuster, 2006). Alex Kotlowitz, *There Are No Children Here: The Story of Two Boys Growing Up in the Other America* (New York: Doubleday, 1991). Kotlowitz describes the life of two boys in a deep poverty area to the east of First Church of the Brethren. Eventually one of the boys, Pharaoh, found a satisfactory life at a private school, Providence St. Mel, just two blocks north of First Church (300).

Men Working has slowly learned to live by faith. The "inter-" has been superseded and even the "intra-" has been laid to rest, though not overcome.

But living by faith means more than sharing a new community. The Galatians spread in Asia Minor. New churches were formed. The intra-community blessed though faith carried out God's mission.[14] Yes, "intra-" differences may be overcome by the grace of God. But Jesus followers working together also overcome differences. Brethren and other "peace churches" have always assumed work camps and mutual disaster teams will unite people who otherwise do not have a common "faith." Writing about Marxists and Christians working together in South America, Thomas A. Lewis argues that there can be "a conception of community based in shared practices even in the absence of shared metanarratives."[15]

So in First Church the BMW travels with its new wheels largely because it has tasks to do. The men discovered they could sing, so they formed a seven-person quartet that sings African-American spirituals every month for the congregation. The men continue to have barbecues to subsidize a college scholarship program for neighborhood youth. And most recently they renovated a neighboring building to house year-round educational programs for college age youth. The intra-community has received God's grace, but it also exists in God's mission. It has wheels that move.

---

[14] G. F. Snyder, *Irish Jesus, Roman Jesus: The Formation of Early Irish Christianity* (Harrisburg: Trinity Press International, 2002) 97.

[15] Thomas A. Lewis, "On the Limits of Narrative: Communities in Pluralisitc Society," *The Journal of Religion* 86 (2006): 55–80. See p. 70.

Proclamation

Careful Worship

CHARLES E. POOLE

It would appear that God takes worship rather seriously; so seriously that Israel's worship around the golden calf actually placed their entire existence in jeopardy, according to Exodus 32. This passage raises a number of intriguing questions. For starters, exactly what was Aaron thinking when he told Moses that the golden calf just sprang up all by itself (Exodus 32:24)? And what about God? Did God really get so angry that God was on the verge of killing the entire congregation (Exodus 32:10)? And what's this about Moses persuading God to change God's mind (Exodus 32:14)? Isn't that a contradiction of 1 Samuel 15:29, which says, "God will not change God's mind?"

Exodus 32 leaves us with several questions we can't answer, and one message we can't miss. The quiet, simple message from that loud, chaotic story is that we should be careful about worship. The trouble in this story started when the people pressured Aaron for something exciting to worship and Aaron, eager to please them, gave them what they wanted. Instead of insisting on the careful worship of God, Aaron responded to popular opinion and created the calf so the people could feel better sooner. The fierceness of God's response ("They have cast for themselves the image of a calf and have worshiped it... Now let me alone...so that I may consume them." Exodus 32:8–10) reminds us that who, and how, we worship matters. That may be the main message for us from the story of the golden calf: the people of God should always be careful about the worship of God.

Careful worship begins in speech that is careful to be truthful about God and with people. To be truthful about God in worship is to say words, sing songs and display symbols that help us think clearly about God. For example, it is a good discipline for us to use no pronouns for God in worship. No he. No she. No him. No her. Why? Because pronouns denote gender and gender is a human category, and we are not worshiping a person, we are worshiping God. That is one small example of careful speech about God.

Careful worship is not only careful to be truthful about God, it is also careful to be truthful with people. No over-promising, no manipulating, no managing people through prayers or sermon. No institutional cheerleading or fundraising in worship. Careful worship that is truthful about God and truthful with people will only use careful speech that is governed and guided by the spirit of Jesus, who is Lord of the Church.

That all sounds simple enough but, practically speaking, how does a congregation practice that kind of careful worship? Here the simple sounding idea of careful worship becomes something less than simple and clear. Indeed, so divergent are the convictions about worship among the people of God that there now exists that dreadful little phrase "the worship wars." (If ever two words did not belong in the same sentence it is the words "worship" and "war.") Different congregations give their praise to God and hear a word from God in very different ways; ways sometimes referred to as liturgical, traditional, or contemporary. But whichever way a church worships, that church should be able to say why they believe that their way of worship is a careful and truthful way of worship that helps people think clearly about the God who was revealed in Jesus.

For example, while I worship God in a variety of settings, the one in which I am most at home is liturgical worship, and I can tell you why: in liturgical worship we follow the perpetually repeated rhythms of the Christian year. Starting with Advent, then Christmastide, then Lent, then Eastertide, the Christian year keeps us moving through the birth, life, death and resurrection of Jesus every year, year after year, for as long as we live. It is a good spiritual discipline to order your life according to the rhythms of the Christian calendar.

In liturgical worship, the Christian calendar is supported by the common lectionary. Following the lectionary binds us to believers throughout the world, all of whom are reading the same Old Testament passage, Psalm, Epistle lesson, or Gospel passage each week. Submitting our own interests and inclinations to the discipline of the worldwide common lectionary is a good hedge against overdone individualism and denominationalism. It reminds us that our church is part of *the* Church.

In liturgical worship, it is typical for the minister to preach in a robe. Just as there are good reasons for living by the liturgical year and the common lectionary, there is also a good reason for preaching in a robe. When a preacher puts on a robe, he or she is wearing the uniform of the church. Just as a soldier surrenders his or her individual interests to the greater cause by putting on a uniform, so the preacher surrenders his or her individual interests to the great universal Church of Jesus Christ by putting on a robe. The robe is a silent symbol of the fact that the preacher represents the church, speaks on behalf of the church, is a servant of the church.

All those elements of liturgical worship; the Christian calendar, the common lectionary, the ministerial robe, are important aids in my careful worship of God, and I have no doubt as to why they are important. However, careful speech requires me to say that I also have no doubt that they are not as important to God as they are to me. I'm pretty sure that God doesn't care whether a person preaches in a robe or a suit or a dress or blue jeans. And while God did give the Hebrew people instructions for high and holy days (Passover, Yom Kippur, Pentecost) Advent, Christmas, and Lent are fourth-century creations of the evolving churches. Plenty of people worship God carefully and truthfully who have never seen a liturgical calendar, a common lectionary, or a ministerial robe. Indeed, I worship regularly in places that are more Pentecostal than liturgical, and I experience the presence of God there as much as I do in "my kind" of service, the very sort of surprise that makes all this not so easy to nail down.

Another reason this is not so easy to talk about, is that it is sometimes difficult to tell the difference between which of our worship preferences are matters of "style," and which are matters of substance. For example, I would say that the presence or absence of national symbols in worship is a matter of theological substance, not worship style. I believe it is best for churches to not display our national symbols, because it is important to keep it clear in people's minds that America is not God's favorite nation. God is the God of the whole world. As I once heard Walter Shurden say, "No nation's flag is big enough to wrap around the cross or the pulpit." Christian symbols—the cross, the pulpit, the altar—don't need to be mixed with national symbols such as the flag and the Pledge. That convergence sends the wrong message. Of course, many churches do display national symbols, while also seeking to worship God carefully. I have no right to criticize that practice, but truthful speech requires me to say that I believe keeping sacred space sacred is not a matter of "worship style," but a matter of theological substance.

To speak carefully and truthfully about the worship of God is not easy. Most difficult of all is to speak clearly about your own convictions regarding the worship of God without speaking unkindly about the ways other people worship God. And, as for those times when we worship in a setting we plan not to like, but find ourselves deeply moved by the presence of God in ways we did not expect, well, that's good for us, isn't it? It reminds us that the mystery of worship is alive, and that we must find a way to talk about different ways of worship that is *judgeless* without being *careless*. I know how I feel when my own way of worship, which tends to be more quiet and orderly, is judged to be "less spiritual" because it is less spontaneous or less visibly emotional. Knowing how troubled I am by that kind of false judgment, I labor to refrain from judging anyone else's way of worship. Having felt the sting of "spiritual" elitism, I don't want to be guilty of "liturgical" elitism, because one brand of elitism is just as unbecoming of Christians as is another. Having said all of that, the fact remains that, by whatever way we Christians construct and order our worship, we must be careful that what we say and sing is true to the spirit of God, the God who brought Israel out of Egypt, the God who was revealed in the words and works of Jesus our Lord.

There are 8,760 hours in a year. If we come to church every Sunday, we spend 52 of those 8,760 hours in Sunday morning worship. For 52 of our 8,760 hours a year we should be able to think carefully about God, speak carefully of God, sing carefully to God, and listen carefully for God. A lifetime of that kind of careful worship will create people of careful speech and careful lives. Careful, truthful worship that resists the temptation to overpromise or overclaim, worship that refuses to play to the grandstands in an effort to excite, manipulate or manage people, will eventually produce people of God who will not exaggerate, lie, spin, cut corners, play fast and loose with the truth, or dance around substitute altars.

That is what careful, truthful worship can do. It can produce people who speak and act and think carefully and truthfully most Mondays because of what they have seen and sung and heard most Sundays.

Amen.[1]

---

[1] For this way of thinking about careful lives formed by careful worship, I am indebted to the influence of Stanley Hauerwas and William Willimon.

I offer this essay in a book honoring Edd Rowell because of the deep and abiding passion Edd and Ruth share for the worship of God.

The Gospel According to Mary Magdalene[1]

BOB SETZER, JR.

John 20:1-18

As surely everyone in the Western Hemisphere knows by now, Mary Magdalene has hit the big time. After nearly 2,000 years as a member of the Gospel's supporting cast, she has catapulted to all-star status. It's like Mary Magdalene competed on *American Idol*...and won! Now she's right up there with Carrie Underwood and Taylor Hicks, gracing the cover of news magazines and generating headlines in the tabloids. Plus Mary Magdalene has spawned one of the best-selling novels of all time, Dan Brown's *The Da Vinci Code*, read by more than 60 million people. During its weekend debut, The *Da Vinci Code* movie generated the second largest box office take in history at $220 million. Only *Star Wars Episode III: Revenge of the Sith* had a bigger opening.

But unlike *Star Wars*, which everyone except for a few UFO enthusiasts knows is science fiction, *The Da Vinci Code* is being taken seriously by a lot of people. And not as

---

[1] The sermon "The Gospel According to Mary Magdalene" spoke to the cause celebre that erupted when *The DaVinci Code* movie came out. As usual, Edd Rowell sent email clippings and commentary that helped me assess that headline making event. His wisdom, integrity, generosity, and wit make him a blessing to many and especially to me.

Being on Edd Rowell's email distribution list is a boon for a working pastor like myself. It's like having an unpaid research assistant providing relevant material and thoughtful commentary on the pressing issues of the day. None of the usual inane email forwards come from Edd; only incisive cyber clippings from one of the most widely read people I know.

entertainment, but as the long repressed but at last revealed "truth" of the Gospel, namely, that Jesus was your run-of-the-mill, all-American boy with a crush on Mary Magdalene. Further, he married her and fathered children, the descendants of whom are now running around somewhere in southern France.

Meanwhile, a corrupt church conspired to keep all this secret, but there are hints aplenty for the enlightened that things are not what they seem. According to Dan Brown, the figure on Jesus' right in Da Vinci's masterpiece, "The Last Supper," is not a young John, the beloved disciple, with peach fuzz on his face, but is actually Mary Magdalene. Somehow this revelation escaped art lovers and scholars alike for the last 500 years.

There are a few occasions when Dan Brown and his wannabes touch down for a glancing bit of truth amid their flights of fancy. Yes, Mary Magdalene generated some interesting legends in Christian tradition. And yes, there are so-called Gnostic gospels written much later than the New Testament that contradict much of the New Testament witness. And yes, the church has often been controlling and even punitive in its relationship to women. But as Robin Griffith-Jones wrote in his book, *The Da Vinci Code and the Secrets of the Temple*, "There have been, in Christian history, more than enough conspiracies and lies and errors; but those imagined in The Da Vinci Code are not among them."[2]

For though interested in a blow-by-blow debunking of *The Da Vinci Code*, I would refer you to Robin Griffith-Jones' excellent book, or to any number of web sites that effectively

[2] Robin Griffith-Jones, *The Da Vinci Code and the Secrets of the Temple* 115. Griffith-Jones is Master of the Temple in London where the infamous Templars of *Da Vinci Code* fame got their start.

refute *The Da Vinci Code's* conspiratorial theories.[3] But personally, I find the Mary Magdalene of the gospels immensely more interesting and radical than the figure Dan Brown has sewn from whole cloth. The biblical Mary Magdalene did not leave her mark on history by becoming a devoted wife and mother, an honorable but hardly remarkable fate. No, the biblical Mary Magdalene left her mark on history by being the first witness of the risen Christ and the first preacher of the world-altering good news: "The Lord is risen! The Lord is risen indeed! I have seen the Lord!"

What does the Bible tell us about Mary Magdalene? First, that she was a native of Magdala, a tiny fishing village on the northwest corner of the Sea of Galilee. Interestingly, Mary of Magdala, unlike most women of the period, is not identified by her relationship to a man. The other Marys we meet in the gospels are identified by their husbands or sons: "Mary the wife of Clopas" or "Mary, the mother of Jesus." But Mary Magdalene is identified not by her husband or son, but by the place of her birth. In other words, she was probably single.

Secondly, we learn in a most interesting passage, Luke 8:1–3, that Mary Magdalene belonged to a small group of women who sometimes traveled with Jesus and the disciples. Luke writes, "Soon afterwards Jesus went on through cities and villages, proclaiming and bringing the good news of the kingdom of God. The twelve were with him—*as well as some women*—who had been cured of evil spirits and infirmities: Mary, called Magdalene, from whom seven demons had gone out, and Joanna, the wife of Herod's steward Chuza, and Susanna, and many others, who provided for them out of their resources." Here's the second shocking, yea radical thing about

---

[3] See for example, http://www.thedavincidialogue.com for articles from an eclectic group of mostly evangelical experts, including Tony Campolo.

Mary Magdalene: Not only was she in all probability *single*, she was also one of Jesus' *female disciples*, a scandalous thing in the ancient world where women were barred from theological study.

Dr. Luke tells us Jesus exorcized seven demons from Mary Magdalene. In the Bible, seven is the number of completion or perfection. That Mary Magdalene was possessed by seven demons means she was utterly in the grip of the Evil One. Granted, many references to exorcism in the New Testament seem to describe what today might be called psychosis or paranoid schizophrenia. But however Mary's exorcism is understood, clearly Jesus delivered her from a terrible plight. Little wonder her devotion to him ran deep and true.

Finally, from Dr. Luke's brief but revealing note, we learn Mary was one of the women who "provided for [Jesus and his followers] out of her resources." In other words, Mary Magdalene was helping bankroll Jesus' operations. She was almost certainly not the repentant prostitute of Christian tradition, but a highborn woman of some means who dropped everything to follow Jesus.

Who then was Mary Magdalene? For all its feminist rhetoric, the Mary Magdalene of Dan Brown's vision is remarkably old fashioned. She is valued for her presumed sexual attractiveness and her ability to bear children. By contrast, the Mary Magdalene of the scriptures is what today we would call a career woman with a well-stocked 401k. And she is not Jesus' *mistress*. She is Jesus' *disciple*, a far more revolutionary role, both then and now.

Fast forward now to the last week of Jesus' life. Matthew tells us that Mary, along with some other women, traveled with Jesus and the disciples to Jerusalem to keep the Passover in

Jerusalem. In chapter 27, verse 55, Matthew paints a moving picture of these women at the cross: "Many women were also there, looking on from a distance; they had followed Jesus from Galilee and had provided for him. Among them were Mary Magdalene, and Mary the mother of James and Joseph, and the mother of the sons of Zebedee." By this point, all the male disciples had cut and run save John, the beloved disciple. It fell to the women to be "last at the cross and first at the tomb."

That brings us to our text for the morning, John's account of the first Easter morning. Matthew, Mark, and Luke mention several other women made the trek with Mary to anoint Jesus' body at the tomb. John focuses his camera shot on Mary only, but since she is the single woman mentioned in every gospel's telling of the first Easter, she is universally credited as being the first woman, indeed, the first *person* to see the risen Christ.

It is clear from John's dramatic account that neither Mary nor anyone else was expecting Easter. She was expecting to subdue the stench of a decaying corpse by anointing it with perfume. What she found instead was an empty tomb: Jesus' body was missing. This fact did not lead her to conclude he had risen, only that someone had moved or stolen the body. Mary then rushed to find help and came back with Peter and John, the beloved disciple, in tow.

Peter and John entered the tomb and examined the evidence with typical male efficiency. Clearly, this was no grave robbery, for Jesus' burial shroud and turban were carefully folded. What grave robber would take time to do that? Still, as to what had happened, they didn't have a clue. After looking things over, Peter rose, dusted himself off, and promptly headed home.

We are told the beloved disciple, the darling of John's gospel, "saw and believed." But exactly what he believed is not clear since the very next verse tells us, "The [disciples] did not yet understand the scripture that [Jesus] must rise from the dead." Perhaps the beloved disciple simply believed Mary's report the tomb was empty. At any rate, after checking out the scene, he promptly left and traipsed after Peter.

In a sense, Peter and John embody the Da Vinci Code way of finding out the truth about Jesus: examine the evidence, make a rational judgement about who Jesus was, what he taught and what became of him, then be on your way. The problem is, such a cool, detached analysis leaves us with a Jesus so depressingly familiar, a Jesus so depressingly *like us:* confused, conflicted, torn, governed more by his passion than his obedience. Truth be told, the Jesus of *The Da Vinci Code*—and most other such attempts to give us the "real Jesus"—only yield a mirror image of ourselves.

But what if the truth about Jesus is not something one can discover by casually examining an empty tomb, much less reading a novel? What if the truth about Jesus is too big, too cosmic, too world-shattering to fit into our accustomed ways of knowing? What if the truth about Jesus is not found primarily through examining evidence but through a soul-wrenching, life-changing encounter? The renowned British intellectual, G. K. Chesterton, rightly observed that truth must be stranger than fiction because "fiction is the creation of the human mind and therefore congenial to it."

Peter and John embody the *Da Vinci Code* way of learning the truth about Jesus, a way that is cool, calculating, and stereotypically male. But Mary shows us another way, for she sees the truth about Jesus not through her head, but through her heart, not through the camera lens but through her tears.

"Woman, why are you weeping?" ask the two angels in the tomb.

"They have taken away my Lord," Mary wails, "and I don't know where they laid him."

No sooner has Mary spluttered the words than she is startled by a stranger from behind. He repeats the angels' question: "Woman, why are you weeping? Whom are you looking for?"

Thinking he must be the gardener—who else would be up at this ungodly hour?—Mary pleads, "Oh sir, if you have taken him away, tell me where you have laid him and I will take him with me."

Then Jesus utters the one word that changes everything, her name: "Mary."

Upon hearing Jesus call her name, the scales fall from Mary's eyes and she sees who is addressing her. "Rabboni!" she cries.

Here, Jesus makes good on a promise from earlier in John's gospel: "The good shepherd calls his sheep by name. The sheep hear his voice and follow him" (10:3). It is as Jesus calls Mary's name that she awakens to his risen life. Her newly quickened faith is not a deduction drawn from dusty evidence; it is a certainty forged in a life-changing encounter with Jesus Christ.

Pastor Jack Hayford paid a hospital call to Carl who was dying of cancer. Carl, a committed Christian, was a much sought-after lighting director in Hollywood. Jack Hayford asked the patient how he was doing and Carl replied, "Pastor Jack, you know when you're in my business, it's the combination of lights, the skill at blending things together in order to create special effects; that's what this job is about."

Then the dying man added, "This morning I woke up and in the quiet of my heart, Jesus spoke to me and said, 'Carl, how would you like to direct a sunset?'"[4]

"Carl!" "Mary!" "Bob!" It is when Jesus, the Risen One, calls our name that we know he is not some figment of an overworked imagination. Rather he is, as Christians in every time and place have proclaimed, God's One and Only Son who fully shared our lives and even our death that he might breath new life, eternal life into our God-starved spirits.

In Michael Green's little book *Who Is This Jesus?*, he confesses to believing for years that Jesus was a great and noble man, but dead as the proverbial doornail. But then, like dawn creeping over the horizon, he began to believe the promise of Easter might actually be true. "And the most momentous consequence of all this?" writes Green. "[Jesus] is still around! …I still recall the force with which this struck me at the time I was beginning to become a disciple of his. If he rose, he must be alive. If he is alive, should I not meet him? And I did."

"Mary, Carl, Michael, Bob!" What is *your* name? Might it be remotely possible the living Christ is calling for you? Of course, to hear him, you'll have to do something far more radical than read *The Da Vinci Code*. You'll have to stop merely examining Jesus and risk loving him.

When Jesus calls Mary's name, she recognizes and clutches him in sobbing relief, holding on for dear life. Gently, Jesus loosens her grip. "Don't cling to me," he tells her. "For I have not yet ascended to my Father. But go to my brothers and

---

[4] TLC, 21 April 2006.

say to them, 'I am ascending to my Father and your Father, to my God and your God.'"

Mary can no longer cling to the old Jesus, the one she knew as rabbi, teacher, master. No, he has forevermore become the crucified and risen one who brings the living God near. Dazed and delirious with joy, Mary of Magdala rushes to where the old boy network is holed up in fear. There, this "Apostle to the apostles" is the first to proclaim the great good news of Easter: "I have seen the Lord!"

Now at last, this woman once possessed by seven demons is fully, unequivocally free: free to shatter the pride and privilege of a patriarchal culture; free to live her life as a blessed daughter of God; free to feel the presence and power of Jesus Christ in the very marrow of her being; free to live forever, not as Jesus' mistress, but in the infinitely more powerful role, as his disciple. For Mary of Magdala has at last experienced the real truth about Jesus. And that truth, *his* truth, has set her free: "For you shall know the truth and the truth shall set you free! ...And if the *Son* sets you free, you shall be free indeed!" (John 8:32, 36).

The tag line of *The Da Vinci Code* movie is "Seek the truth." Indeed, that is your charge, not as mere moviegoers but as disciples and would-be disciples of Jesus: "Seek the truth." Just don't mistake the truth about Jesus for some special knowledge reserved for the privileged few. Such special knowledge is the stuff of Gnostic novels, both ancient and modern.

But Mary's tears revealed no superior knowledge. What her tears revealed was a superior love. For then, as now, such love yielded the truth about Jesus; that he, God's One and Only Son, lived, died, and rose again that he might call *your* name and set you free.

The Gospel According to Judas[1]

BOB SETZER, JR.

Luke 22:1–6; Matthew 27:1–5

According to an old legend, when Jesus returned to heaven, God embraced him with a bear hug. "Good to have you back," said the Father.

"Good to be back," said the Son.

"I'm sorry for your suffering," said God, eyes clouding with pain. "I hope I didn't let you down."

Jesus shook his head. "No, Father. You warned me it would be rough."

"So tell me, son. What was the worst of your sufferings? Was it the beating, the thorns, the nails?"

"No," said Jesus, wincing at the memory. "It was the kiss."

---

[1] The sermon "The Gospel According to Judas" drew in part on Edd's excellent sermon, "Failure Need Not Be Fatal" *(Finding God in the Rest of the Story*, Macon, Georgia: Smyth & Helwys Publishing, Inc., 1998, p. 11ff.). Not only is Edd a modern renaissance man; he is an outstanding preacher. He takes carefully distilled theological truth and turns it into a potent word from God. Whenever Edd preaches at our place, the First Baptist Church of Christ at Macon, hearers of every theological stripe and stylistic preference give him rave reviews.

That is in part because we know Edd as a man of deep, abiding faith who is passionately committed to the life and witness of our church. To hear Edd sing "His Eye Is On the Sparrow," with his lovely wife Ruth accompanying him at the piano, is to savor the tenderest and most truthful of confessions.

Of all those who failed Jesus in the clutch, Judas' blunder was the most calculated and disappointing. The other disciples betrayed Jesus due to a loss of courage. For Judas, it was a decision. Little wonder no one in Christian history has been so hated and despised.

But I've sometimes wondered: who was Judas before he was a scoundrel? Was he a traitor from the beginning or did he grow into the role? In John's Gospel, the answer seems to be Judas was a bad apple from the start. But Matthew, Mark, and Luke all treat Judas with a little more sympathy.

Matthew, for example, tells us that following the crucifixion, Judas was so overcome with remorse he hung himself. And Luke notes that only as the end drew near did "Satan *enter* into Judas." In other words, the Prince of Darkness had lurked nearby from the beginning, like a deadly virus waiting to infect its victim. But only as the end drew near did Satan get the opening he'd hoped for.

Recently, the newly translated *Gospel of Judas* has put Judas back in the headlines. This ancient document, lost for 1,700 years, was found by an illiterate garlic farmer in an Egyptian cave. After thirty years of being bought and sold in the shadowy world of biblical antiquities, this crumbling relic was finally secured by *National Geographic*. Now, after several years of painstaking effort, scholars have restored 80 percent of the manuscript. The story it tells is scandalous and shocking, namely, that Jesus orchestrated his death using Judas as a foil, and that salvation is found in mastering the secret teaching Jesus entrusted to Judas.

This heretofore missing Gospel, *The Gospel of Judas*, was not unknown in the church's early centuries. In fact, it was denounced as fiction and heresy, which probably explains why it disappeared in the first place. Further, as a source of reliable information about either Judas or Jesus, the *Gospel of Judas* is suspect. It was written a century or so after the New Testament Gospels. As Ben Witherington of Asbury Theological Seminary observed, thinking *The Gospel of Judas* gives us the *real* story of Judas, "Is like saying a document written 150 years after George Washington died tells us the inside truth about George Washington."

Still, I suspect while this ancient Gospel is mostly the work of a fertile religious imagination, it does contain a kernel of truth. And the kernel of truth is this: Judas was guilty of a tragic miscalculation. He may well have betrayed Jesus expecting not Jesus' death but his triumph. Hence, his betrayal, as awful as it was, may have been inspired by a misguided loyalty rather than a faltering love.

Again, to take Luke's spin on the story, it was in the last week of Jesus' life that Satan *entered* into Judas. So what pushed Judas over the edge, permitting Satan to have his way with him? The hint of an answer may lie in Judas' surname: *Iscariot.* The name is connected to the Greek word, "*sikarios,*" means "dagger- bearer." The *Sikarios* were a guerrilla band waging warfare against the Romans, a sort of first-century French resistance. As a member of that radical sect, Judas, like many of his contemporaries, expected Jesus to oust the Romans and establish God's kingdom on earth.

But then on Wednesday of Holy Week, Jesus was dining at the house of Simon the leper when a woman anointed his head with expensive perfume. According to Matthew, *all* the disciples were outraged by this excess, although John's Gospel mentions only Judas. Jesus defended the woman's action, saying she was preparing him for his burial. Apparently, this incident, along with the Jesus' comment about his impending burial, convinced Judas that Jesus was throwing in the towel. In both Matthew and Mark, Judas leaves immediately after the woman's anointing of Jesus to plot his betrayal.

And yet it is just possible Judas intended not so much to betray Jesus, as to force his hand. After all, just days before, Jesus entered Jerusalem in triumph with untold thousands of glad hosannas ringing in his ears. Why then make peace with his approaching death? If Judas could but provoke a crisis, the masses would surely flock to Jesus' cause.

And truth be told, Judas wasn't the last to think he knew better than Jesus. Who among us has not made certain adjustments in order to get by in the "real world"? Have we never resorted to deceit and manipulation to get our way, rather than waiting on a Lord who, we feared, might never show up? The temptation to trust ourselves and our street smarts more than Jesus, is not unique to Judas. He may have set the mold for this particular defection, but all of us have followed after him.

Helmut Thieleke was a German pastor of the confessing church during the terrible days of the Third Reich. Later, as he preached the gospel to a war-ravaged nation, he observed that Satan led Germany astray not by appealing to base motives, but to high ones. The Third Reich was built on patriotism, discipline, and sacrifice. But the Prince of Darkness took those lofty ideals and twisted them to terrible ends.

This, I think, is what happened to Judas. His high ideals were turned to terrible ends because he trusted his own wits more than he trusted Jesus. He led Jesus' enemies to the Master, fully expecting Jesus to sound the call to arms. As Judas pressed his lips against his master's cheek, his grip tightened about the dagger in his cloak, making ready to lunge at the temple guards. And when Peter drew his sword and severed a soldier's ear, Judas lustily anticipated a bloody rout of the high priest's forces.

But then Jesus commanded Peter, "Put your sword away! Am I not to drink the cup the Father has given me?" Judas' heart sank. Clearly, Jesus was intent on going through with this mad scheme to die at the hands of his enemies. So Judas ran for his life, as did all the disciples, until shivering and sobbing in some dark hole of shame, his world came crashing in on him.

Judas' realization that his betrayal spelled the end for Jesus was a pain too great to bear. Desperate to set things right, he ran to the conspirators who hired him. Flinging his 30 pieces of silver at their feet, the anguish of Judas' heart came pouring out: "I have sinned in betraying innocent blood!"

"What is that to us?" they answered with icy cynicism. "See to it yourself."

So Judas did. He went out and hung himself, trying to atone for his sins.

Judas didn't live to see that Jesus died atop Calvary's mountain, so neither Judas nor we would have to do our unblessed dying atop some God-forsaken hill. Instead, Jesus stepped into the darkness created by our defections and betrayals and died there for the sins of the world. And by the mercy of God, that death was not the end but the beginning. It was not the failure of a grand scheme, but the fulfillment of a divine design. For in the death of his Son, God made atonement for the sins of Judas, and for us, betrayers all.

Among mountain climbers, the most important climber is the one holding the rope. When a climber slips and falls, the person holding the safety rope is the victim's only hope. As the spiraling tether shoots through the anchor man's hands, it burns through his gloves and into his flesh. It takes consummate courage to hold on in the face of such pain. But many a falling victim has been saved, because, at great cost to himself, his rope man wouldn't let go.

Judas thought Jesus was the victim atop Golgotha's mountain. He didn't see that by the grace of God, Jesus was the rope man. At infinite cost to himself, Jesus refused to let go of sinners like Judas—and sinners like me—in desperate need of forgiveness. Even when the burden of the world's sin tore into his very flesh, Jesus wouldn't let go. Instead, he clung to all those who would someday look to him in faith and devotion. And that is why his death was not the great debacle Judas feared, but the laying of the cornerstone of an eternal kingdom.

Judas' real betrayal was not that he failed Jesus; he was hardly alone in that. No, Judas' real betrayal was that he didn't trust Jesus enough to ask his forgiveness. Instead, he resorted to suicide, "a permanent solution to a temporary problem." Had he only waited for the light of Christ's Easter triumph, Judas could have awakened to the dawn of a new day as God's forgiven, restored, and cherished child.

In a touching comment, an early church father said Judas committed suicide in a desperate bid to go to Hades, the realm of the dead, to seek out Jesus and beg for forgiveness.

Fortunately, we need not go to such extremes. Jesus is here even now, inviting us back into the healing light of his presence, even though like Judas, we keep getting lost in the darkness of our shame and defections. Jesus already *died* for our sins, so we need not go on punishing ourselves as though we had to pay for them yet again. At the cross, Jesus held on to us, even though time after time, we let go of him. Now all that remains is for us to look to him in love and in longing and ask for the forgiveness and new life he died to give.

Scrawled on the mirror of a rest room in San Francisco was the graffiti message, "Judas, come home all is forgiven!"

Ray Anderson, a professor of theology at Fuller Seminary, paused and wondered, "A bit of wishful thinking, or does that crudely scrawled hope express the deepest truth of the gospel?"

In struggling with that question, Anderson came to believe anew in the extravagance of God's grace in Jesus Christ. Eventually, he penned his own response to the graffiti affirmation. It was and is his book, *The Gospel According to Judas.* The subtitle? *Judas, Come Home All Is Forgiven.*

I cannot reflect upon that scandalous, yet liberating notion, that even *Judas* is invited to come home to God's grace, and with him me, and with him, you, without hearing the strains of the old gospel hymn, "Come home, come home, ye who are weary, come home. Earnestly, tenderly, Jesus is calling. Calling, O *Judas*, come home."

"Come home from that God-forsaken hilltop where you trying to atone for your own sins."

"Come home from all that anxious pretending, trying to cover up a shame that won't let you go."

"Come home from the devil's lie that your sin is too heinous to be forgiven, and let the grace of Jesus Christ set you free."

With Judas, we really can come home from the far country of our worst treacheries and betrayals, for atonement has already been made, and all, *all* is forgiven."

I don't know what happened to Judas on the far side of his suicide. I want to believe Jesus went and found him, as Judas shivered in the darkness and shame of his desperation. And there Jesus put his arms about this desolate man, pulled him close, and said, "Judas, come home. All is forgiven."

But whether or not that happened to Judas, I know it can happen to you. For even now, Jesus is present, inviting, urging, imploring you to come home to God's grace made radiant in his life and etched in red at his death. For on the mirror of our desperation, where we find ourselves staring into endless loops of self-loathing, Jesus has scribbled the message, "Come home, come home. All is forgiven."

That's the gospel. That's the good news. I'd *like* to believe that's the *Gospel According to Judas.* And pray God, that's the *Gospel According to You.*

Into the Wilderness

MARC A. JOLLEY

Exodus 13:17–23

I.

If, in 1963, after Martin Luther King, Jr., had given his "I have a dream" speech someone had told him that at the turn of the twenty-first century that not only had black men and women been voting their convictions for three decades but many had been elected to positions from Congress to the Supreme Court, that integration in the school systems was a reality, that a program called affirmative action was not only in place but demanded constant attention, that the only American-born, living Nobel Prize winner for literature, namely Toni Morrison is an African American, that fifty years after he broke baseball's racial barriers that Jackie Robinson is remembered as a hero, that February is Black History month, that if told all of this and much much more, would that be the "dream" fulfilled, would that be the promised land he would refer to the night before his death?

Likewise, if someone asked the children of Israel while they were leaving Egypt, if their cries for deliverance had been answered, would they have said yes? After years of bondage under a Pharaoh who did not know Joseph, would the Israelites think that their promised land lay in the near distance?

The answer to both of these inquiries would likely have been "Yes." Compared with the way African Americans lived and were treated in the 1960s and the way that opportunities have risen since, King may well have said, "It is finished." But as we all know, the dream has yet to be fulfilled. Racism has not gone away, and while many things are better between blacks and whites, racism has taken on a new form. Just as the Borg aliens in *Star Trek: The Next Generation* can adapt to enemy fire and develop new ways of deflecting it, so too racism. For every two steps we make in the right direction, it deflects us in finding a way to continue as a major threat to our society. It absorbs every attempt at making peace and uses it against us. While integration in the school system was a natural progression of bringing the two races together, it has been met with the rise of gangs, an explosion of private schools, and the use of home-schooling. Some way or other, people find a way to avoid the other race. Some way or other, we have a way of prolonging our entrance into the promised land. We prefer to live in the wilderness.

II.

It all began with Abram and his wife Sarai. As sure as Sarai was barren, she was destined to become pregnant. Every time a woman is pronounced as barren in the Old Testament, she is about to have a child. Abram and Sarai come from a far country to a land of strangers and strange surroundings. Miraculously they had a son, and named him Isaac, meaning laughter. Isaac grew up, married, and had twin sons named Esau and Jacob. After typical brother squabblings, they went their separate ways. Esau, the older brother, stayed home and helped his family with the farm while Jacob left seeking romance and fortune and found both. Four wives and twelve sons later, Jacob came back to the land where Abraham had started it all.

But more family squabbles interrupted their life. Jacob's favorite son Joseph was stripped of his Technicolor dream coat, was sold into slavery, and wound up in an Egyptian jail. So far, from the near death of Abraham at the hands of the Pharoah, the near sacrifice of Isaac, the near rape of Sarah and Rebekah, the near death of Jacob at the hands of his brother Esau, and now the selling of Joseph into a life of slavery in Egypt, one must ask the question: is this what God intended?

And now, with Joseph under chains in Egypt, Jacob under tears of sorrow in Canaan, what would happen to this family that was supposed to become as numerous as the stars of the sky? To use terms only students can understand and we professors and administrators can only remember with shivers, Joseph pulled an "all-nighter" and BSed his way out of jail. Joseph had gifts and used them to gain not only his freedom, but also rose to such fame that the Pharaoh made Joseph his secretary of agriculture, administering all of the farming and storing of food for the country.

And while the popular saying "time has a way of healing wounds," it is also true that time has a way of enabling people to forget, for either the good or bad. The family of Jacob had settled in Egypt while Joseph was alive, for there was a famine in the "promised land." The third such famine since Abraham had arrived there and the fifth time the major character had left the "promised land." Is this what God intended?

Life carried on and one day the people woke up and they found themselves 200 years beyond Joseph and now they were outright slaves. While God had promised Abraham that he would father a great nation and that this land, the land of Canaan, would be for his family, his children's children's children now found themselves bound in a foreign land. They cried out for help, and after a time, God heard them. God chose Moses, born of Hebrew parents and raised by Pharoah's daughter, one of the great humorous ironies in all of Scripture, to deliver the Israelites from their bondage. After killing an Egyptian guard, Moses escapes to another land, not Canaan, and settles down with a new wife and a respectable, albeit smelly job watching and raising sheep. Just when our hero feels relaxed, the same God who called Abraham, the same God who covenanted with Isaac, the same God who wrestled with Jacob, the same God who empowered Joseph with the ability to interpret dreams, called to Moses from a bush on top of a mountain. God never calls us when we expect it, and he never asks us to do what we want. Rather, he calls us when we are comfortable, just when we think all is well, and things are going well.

Moses did what God asked, but he did so reluctantly. He went to Pharaoh and eventually led the Hebrews out of the iron fist of slavery. Using everything from blood to grasshoppers, Moses utilized God's power over nature to reveal God's power over the universe. After the first born of the Egyptians are killed, then Pharaoh, who by now must have wished he had remembered who Joseph was, lets the people go.

The Hebrews had questioned Moses early, but at this point must have been full of excitement that the day of freedom was close at hand. Finally, after hundreds of years, they would be going home to the land of their ancestors, the land of Israel. They would at last be free.

But freedom has its price. Following the Civil War, slaves suddenly found themselves free in the South, but jobs were non-existent. Help from Southern whites was even more scarce. Forty acres and a mule was just that. Money to buy seed was not to be found. And per human nature, one response to the free black was the rise of white supremacists who vowed that while slavery was illegal, they were not obliged to make the free black welcome. Terrorism wore a white hood, yet the former slaves were free.

Like the children of Israel who followed Moses out of slavery, African Americans followed Abraham Lincoln into freedom with the Emancipation Proclamation. Like Israel, the former slaves of the South lost their deliverer just before the promise was completely fulfilled. Andrew Johnson and Joshua had similar fates, that while both had certain gifts, filling the shoes of their predecessors was not one of them.

III.

And so the Israelites left Egypt. They went into the wilderness, uncertain of their future, but certain of their past. Slavery was something to leave behind. Yet, upon entering the wilderness, they began to question their future. Did God intend that we go hungry? Did God intend that we die of thirst? Did God intend that the Egyptians catch us here on the shore of the sea and bury our corpses in the sea? What is freedom? Is it free from the slavery of another person, or is it freedom to starve to death? Is not the real slavery that of dependence on food and water?

And yet, every time the people needed, God provided. Manna, water, shade, rest, directions. I was looking at a friend's photographs of the Holy Land, and while looking a one shot of the desert near Jordan, it occurred to me the problem Moses faced. The people had been raised on the stories of the homeland, a land full of milk and honey. Yet none of them had ever seen it. After leaving Egypt and upon entering the wilderness, the photograph made me ask the question, what was Moses' response when he saw the wilderness that awaited them? Did he say something like, "This is going to be harder than I thought?" or "We should have stayed in Egypt"?

Probably neither. Moses was the only Israelite who had ever been in the wilderness. No one else had been outside of Egypt. Moses knew something else. He knew that the promised land was not a place that could be reached with miles of walking. But it is a place only found after one has journeyed the wilderness. With God leading by day and by night, the Israelites had to simply follow. They never liked this role. They wanted to be home now. They were not willing to cross their wilderness to reach the promise. Like a freshman who thinks that college will never be over, the Israelites did not see the wilderness as a means to an end, but the end itself.

One only needs to look at the history of Israel and one can plainly see that the land of Canaan has never been and is not today a land of peace and promise. Like Israel, Christians today live in the wilderness between our old way of life as slaves to sin and the promise of heavenly peace. The Wilderness is our home while on earth. Many African Americans remember the days when segregation was gospel and lynchings were spectator sports, and yet even today, with things so much better, hatred and racism have taken on new guises and keep the promised land from materializing. Like slaves following the Civil War who found themselves free and yet unwelcome nearly everywhere, the wilderness was their home.

So where is the promised land? As for Israel it is so with us. It is not a place where one can say, "Look, there it is," or "Wait, its over there." Rather, the promised land is found in the wilderness. It is where we meet God in the bush. And when we meet God, God says two things: (1) Remove your shoes, for the ground you are standing on is holy; and (2) I am the light of the world. Whoever follows me will never walk in darkness, but will have the light of life.

This side of Easter, once we have met God at the bush, we become like Moses and the disciples: we stand up, go to those in prison and proclaim the release of the captives, and bring them to the bush, to the light of the world, the light that never fails.

Confessions of a Soldier

MARC A. JOLLEY

Mark 15:16–47[1]

The war in Iraq gives us special images to reflect on this day. The image of soldiers and civilians are fresh in our minds. Since the war began, *Newsweek* magazine has provided sound coverage. In one photo spread that first week, they published several photographs of soldiers in the act of religious devotion. One soldier was sitting at a table. The tray of food was before him with the usual foods. His elbows were on the table, his hands holding each other. His head was bowed. The images in *Newsweek* have been with me for the past five weeks.

On television, we saw an Iraqi family taken from their home and a young girl crying, on her knees, not sure whether she should hold her hands over her head in surrender or put her hands under her chin to pray.

Soldiers are everywhere. Even in the New Testament. In the Gospel of Mark, we read of a centurion who was present at the death of Jesus. Briefly, a Roman legion was made up of 6,000 soldiers. A centurion was in charge of 100, so there were roughly 60 centurions for each legion. The centurion had to be of Italian birth and Roman citizenship, and they were in charge of not only training the soldiers in his command, but of instilling in each one of them the "Roman spirit."

---

[1] Delievered originally on Good Friday, 18 April 2003 at Highland Hills Baptist Church.

Centurions in the New Testament had varied roles. Julius, a centurion, had the task of taking Paul to Rome (Acts 27:1). One certain Cornelius converted to Christianity in the Book of Acts (10:1–11:18). Most remarkably, a centurion in Matthew 8 (5–13) is the true example of faith when Jesus heals the centurion's servant only by the word and by faith rather than going to him to lay his hands on the sick man.

In the Gospel of Mark, however, the centurion's announcement at the cross is to be seen in a different, more amazing light. In the Gospel of Mark, those closest to Jesus never really understand who Jesus is. The disciples are very ignorant in Mark. They hear Jesus speak parables and then later when they are alone with him they ask him what he meant. In Mark 8, Jesus asks them who they think he is. Peter comes close when he says that Jesus is the Messiah. But a few verses later we know that Peter was thinking about a Davidic-like messiah when Jesus refers to Peter as "Satan."

At the arrest of Jesus in the garden the night before his death, the disciples run away, and only moments before Peter claims that he would never leave Jesus. Even at the tomb on Easter morning, the women go there and are afraid and leave before finding the truth. Those closest to Jesus in the Gospel of Mark never get it. They never perceive who Jesus is. Physically, geographically, they are very close to him, yet they do not have the slightest idea who Jesus really is.

Add to this that the Jewish religious leaders (the ones in the Gospel, but not all were this way—the Pharisees of Hillel, for example)—political, religious, scholarly, and priestly—never accept Jesus: instead they are trying to find ways to get rid of him from the beginning.

In the Gospel of Mark, Jesus heals some blind people. The irony is that those who are blind come to see Jesus for who he is, but those who were not blind and see Jesus don't recognize him at all. Those who cannot see physically can see spiritually, but those who can see physically are blind spiritually. The insiders—the disciples and the religious leaders—are ignorant of who Jesus is.

The contrary view is seen through the "outsiders." Gentiles like the centurion, a woman suffering a lifelong illness, and demon-possessed individuals are the only ones who seem to catch on to who Jesus truly is. The demons shout out for mercy because they recognize him. The centurion has faith that Jesus did not find in all Israel. With these Gentiles, the only other announcement of who Jesus is comes at the baptism when God says, "You are my son, with whom I am well pleased."

Do you remember the movie *Big*. It is a wonderful film about a twelve-year-old boy who is tired of being twelve and wants to be an adult. He goes to the boardwalk with a friend, and a fortune-telling machine grants him his wish. He wakes up the next morning a grown man. He moves into New York City and gets a job as a computer analyst at MacMillan Toys. The next thing you know he is an executive giving advice on new toys. He is an outsider who comes to the boring executive discussions of what kinds of toys kids will like. His outside perspective brings truth and honesty. He, the outsider, is the only one in the room who understands kids. Fortunately, the president of the company recognizes this and is "converted" to this boy's ideas.

As the Gospel of Mark stands, the pinnacle of the story is the passion narrative. The arrest, trial, and crucifixion of Jesus is where Mark is taking us from the first words of the Gospel. In our text for this evening, we read of Pilate, soldiers, and a centurion in the final moments of Jesus' life. Pilate passes sentence on Jesus for treason. Anyone claiming to be the "Son of God," or the "King of the Jews" was a traitor to the emperor and swift execution was the sentence. We must remember that in Rome the emperor was called and referred to as the son of god. There was no king but the emperor. Jesus was nothing to Pilate. Pilate had crucified thousands during his reign. What was one more?

The soldiers took Jesus and mocked him, knelt down to him, gave him a crown. While the centurion is not mentioned, he must have been there since he will be the one to carry out the sentence. He was in the garden when Jesus calms his disciples' fears, when he heals the servant's severed ear, and when Jesus is abandoned by everyone when he is arrested.

Jesus is taken to Golgotha, his cross carried part of the way by, yes, an outsider, Simon of Cyrene. The cross is in place, Jesus is nailed to it securely, and the treasonous charge of "King of the Jews" is placed on the cross. Anyone who claims to be the son of God or to be a king will meet the same fate. Also, anyone who claims to accept this man as king or as God's son will be put to death in a similar manner.

While on the cross, Jesus cries out for God. This is the darkest moment in history of the world. When Jesus says to his father in heaven, "My God, my God, why have you forsaken me?" all hope is gone. With the death of untold millions of innocents, this darkness has been repeated throughout the centuries.

Then, in the way that only God could do it, there is a miracle. There is a conversion. The centurion is facing Jesus who hangs dead on the cross, and the soldier proclaims, "Truly this man was God's Son." That is our image. That is our photograph. A soldier with a sword at his side, in full regalia, becoming a traitor to the empire. It's the moment when Darth

Vader hurls the emperor into the abyss. It is a moment of triumphant faith. Good triumphs over evil. Truth rises above untruth. There stands the soldier, his allegiance wavering, his head swimming. He looks up at a man who had healed people, cast out demons, made the blind see, raised people from the dead, who dared to teach that the love—not hate—of God and of neighbor was the only philosophy and politics worth dying for, a man who taught his followers to go the extra mile. How conflicted this soldier must have felt. There he was, standing in front of a dead man on a cross who had asked God to forgive these soldiers and this world because they knew not what they were doing. The centurion stood there, watching the blood flow down that cross. It was the blood of a man who taught, "Blessed are the peacemakers, for they shall be called the children of God."

"Truly this man was God's Son."

And now, he was dead.

Edmon Lewin Rowell, Jr.

Senior Editor, Mercer University Press,
Mercer University, Macon, Georgia

Vital

b. 5 February 1937, Covington County (Andalusia), Alabama

Education

AB 1961, Howard College (now Samford University)
BD 1966, MDiv 1972, Southeastern Baptist Theological Seminary

Vocation

US Army, staff sergeant, 1954–1957 (eighteen months, Korea)
Pastor, Letohatchee Alabama Baptist Church
Pastor, Steep Creek Baptist Church, Hope Hull (AL), 1958–1961
Night manager, Holiday Inn and Plantation Inn (Raleigh NC), 1961–1963
Interim Minister of Music, North Rocky Mount Baptist Church (Rocky Mount NC), 1963
Interim pastor, St. Stephens Baptist Church (SC), 1964
Interim pastor, Woodlawn Baptist Church (Wake Forest NC), 1965
Pastor, Critz Baptist Church (Critz VA), May 1966–November 1969

Pastor, Mayo Baptist Church (Spencer VA), May 1966–July 1969

Pastor, Clover Baptist Church (Clover VA), November 1969–October 1971

Pastor, Lee Street Baptist Church (Danville VA), October 1971–May 1975

Adjunct instructor in religion, Averett College, 1972–1974

Pastor, Livingston First Baptist Church (AL), May 1975–July 1980

Adjunct instructor, University College, Mercer, 1990–

*Senior editor, Mercer University Press, August 1980–

Interim pastor: Porterfield, February 1981–January 1882; Mt. Zion (Danville VA), February–May 1982; Mt. Pleasant (Gordon), May–July 1982; Parkway, July 1982–April 1983; Glenwood Hills, July 1983–May 1984; Shurlington, July–November 1984; Plentitude (Gray), December 1984–June 1985; Houston Heights, June 1985–February 1986; Porterfield, March–October 1986; Morningside, October 1986–July 1987; Plentitude, April–November 1995; Brown Memorial (Wrightsville, December 1995–April 1996; Russellville Baptist Church (GA), November 1997–July 1998; Providence Baptist Church), March–May 1999; Russellville Baptist Church (GA), July 1999–May 2001, July 2002–January 2003

Supply pastor: including Avondale, Bethesda, Beulah (Sparta, Central, Cherokee Heights, College Hill (Mt. Vernon), Cordele First Baptist Church, Fitzgerald Baptist Fellowship, Forsyth First Baptist Church, Fort Valley First Baptist Church, Greensboro First Baptist Church, Highland Hills (Macon GA), Hillsboro, Immanuel, Lizella, Log Cabin, Macon First Baptist Church (home church; GA), Midway, Montezuma, Savannah First Baptist Church

(GA), Sharpsburg, Southside, Tabernacle, Thomaston Road, Trinity (Thomaston), Warner Robins First Baptist Church (GA), Wesleyan Drive, Wynnbrook (Columbus GA)

PROFESSIONAL ASSOCIATIONS

Society of Biblical Literature, 1966–
American Academy of Religion, 1972–
National Association of Baptist Professors of Religion, 1975–
International Institute for the Renewal of Gospel Studies, 1985–

FAMILY

Wife

Ruth Carolyn Teague Rowell (Ruth)
b. 13 July 1940, m. 21 December 1963
AA 1960, Mars Hill College. AB cum laude 1962, Furman University; graduate studies, Southeastern Baptist Theological Seminary, 1962–1963.
Private piano teacher, 1963–
Church-related: min. of music and youth, Newfound Baptist Church (Leicester NC), 1963; founder-director, Lee Street Singers and director, children's music program, Lee Street Baptist Church (Danville VA), 1972–1975; minister of music and founder-director of "Thursday's Children" (Christian education program—music, mission studies, directed recreation), First Baptist Church (Livingston AL), 1975–1980; church pianist, First Baptist Church (Macon GA), July 1982–; graded choir coordinator/director, First Baptist Church Macon, August 1982–

Professional Associations
National Guild of Piano Teachers
American Music Teachers National Association
Morning Music Club (past president)

Children
Margaret Elizabeth (Beth) McGinnis

b. 1 November 1969, m. Scott McGinnis 20 June 1992

BMus summa cum laude, Samford University, 1991. MMus, Texas Christian University, 1995. PhD, University of North Carolina, Chapel Hill, 2003

Instructor, School of Music, Birmingham-Southern University, 1991–1992; instructor, School of Music, Samford University, 1992–1993; instructor, School of Music, Texas Christian University, 1995–1996; staff accompanist, Duke School of Music, 1996–2002; minister of music, Ephesus Baptist Church (Durham NC), 2001–2002; instructor, School of Music, Samford University, 2002–

Rebecca Ruth (Rebecca) Cooke

b. 1 December 1971, m. David Cooke 22 March 1997.

BMus, Samford University, 1994. MMus, School of Music, University of Georgia, 1997 PhD candidate (ABD), University of Georgia

Graduate assistant, School of Music, University of Georgia, 1995–1998. Private clarinet and piano teacher, 1994–

Edmon Lewin III (Ed or Edmon)

b. 8 April 1974, m. Jacqueline Colavita 7 June 1997

BMus, Samford University (Music Education), 1997

Instrumental director, Lakeside Baptist Church (Birmingham AL), 1995–1997. Private trumpet teacher,

1995–. Band director, Central High School, 1997–2000. Post-graduate at University of Indiana, 2000–2002. Financial advisor, Ameriprise Financial (Indianapolis IN), 2005–

Grandchildren
Caroline and *Beau Cooke*
William and *Kate McGinnis*
Sofia Rowell and another Rowell on the way

PUBLICATIONS

Books

Acts (Part 1) and *Acts (Part 2)*. Bible Book Study Commentary 1/3 and 1/4. Nashville: Convention Press, 1979, 1980.

Apostles—Jesus' Special Helpers. BibLearn series. Nashville; Mountain View CA: Broadman Press; Pacific Press, 1979.

Baptist Summit (Macon GA: Mercer University Press, September 2006). Preface by Edmon Rowell.

Eerdmans Dictionary of the Bible. Grand Rapids MI: Eerdmans, 2000. Edmon contributed "Cendebeus," "Hor," "Leaven," and "Sojourner."

Finding God in the Rest of the Story. Macon GA: Peake Road (Smyth & Helwys Publishing), 1998.

"A Good Example" (excerpt).*Formations Perspectives* (January–April 1999): 9.

"Looking for God" (excerpt). *Formations Perspectives* (September–December 1998): 11.

Mercer Commentary on the Bible. Watson E. Mills and Richard F. Wilson, general editors. Roger A. Bullard, Joel F. Drinkard, Jr., Walter Harrelson, and Edgar V. McKnight, area editors. Macon: Mercer University Press, 1994.

Edmon served as Mercer Press's senior editor on the project and a contributor: "First Esdras," "Third Maccabees," and "Fourth Maccabees."

Mercer Dictionary of the Bible. Watson E. Mills, general editor. Roger A. Bullard, Joel F. Drinkard, Jr., Walter Harrelson, and Edgar V. McKnight, associate editors. Rollin S. Armour, Edmon L. Rowell, Jr., and Richard F. Wilson, assistant editors. Macon GA: Mercer University Press, 1990. Edmon also contributed "Aaronites," "Abijah," "A Biblical 'Calendar,'" "Brass/Bronze," "Canaan, Inhabitants of," "Dedication, Feast of," "English Bible Family Tree," "Ezra/Esdras, Fifth and Sixth," "Flint," "Gehenna," "Hell," "Hinnom, Valley of," "Samaria/Samaritans," "Scepter," "Sea," "Slavery in the Old Testament," "Superscription, Title," "The Synoptic Problem: Two Proposed Solutions," "Weights and Measures."

"What the Bible Says about Stuff" (excerpt). *Baptists Today* 16/11 (November 1998): 25, 28.

Articles/Essays

"I'm Glad You're Here...." *People* 3/10 (July 1973): 20–28.

"The Book." *The Student* 53/3 (December 1973): 12–16.

"The Biblical Idea of 'Soul.'" *Proclaim* 4/3 (April 1974): 26–28.

"The Holy Bible." *Sunday School Lesson Illustrator* 1/3 (Spring 1975): 33–37.

"Preach the Word." *Proclaim* 6/2 (January 1976): 26–27.

"Philippi of Macedonia: Beachhead in Europe." *Sunday School Lesson Illustrator* 4/3 (Spring 1978): 38–45. Reprinted in *The Best of the Illustrator. The Journeys of Paul*. Nashville: BSSB/SBC, 1990. Pp. 45–49.

"The Bishop Lists of Rome." *Sunday School Lesson Illustrator* 5/2 (Winter 1979): 17–19.

"A Lamb...Slain." *Biblical Illustrator* (formerly *Sunday School Lesson Illustrator*) 8/3 (Spring 1982): 78–79.

"Jesus' Postresurrection Appearances to His Disciples." *Biblical Illustrator* 13/2 (Winter 1987): 33–34.

"The University Press as 'Religious' Publisher." *The Council of Societies for the Study of Religion Bulletin* 17/4 (November 1988): 77–79.

"The Brook Kidron." *Biblical Illustrator* 16/2 (Winter 1990): 42–52.

"King Joash." *Biblical Illustrator* 18/4 (Summer 1992): 32–36.

"You Did It to/for Me, Amos 5:1–17." In *Interpreting Amos for Preaching and Teaching*, ed. Cecil P. Staton, Jr. Kerygma and Church series. Macon GA: Smyth & Helwys, 1995. 65–77

"A First-Century Ephesian House." *Biblical Illustrator* 21/2 (Winter 1996): 61–63.

"First-Century Spain." *Biblical Illustrator* 22/2 (Spring 1996): 43–46.

"Gentiles." *Biblical Illustrator* 24/2 (Winter 1997–1998): 43–46.

Curriculum Materials

"Applying the Bible Passages." *Adult Life and Work Lesson Annual, 1975-1976*. Nashville: Convention Press, 1975. 387–88, 393–94, 401, 407–408.

"Applying the Bible Passages" (Sunday school lessons for 24, 31 July and 7, 14 August 1977). *Adult Life and Work Lesson Annual, 1976–1977*. Nashville: Convention Press, 1976. 336–37, 344–45, 352–53, 360–61.

"Teaching Young Adults" (twenty-one Sunday school lesson plans for 5 December 1976–24 April 1977). *The Adult Teacher* 23/1–3 (October 1976–June 1977).

"Planning for Bible Study—Convention Uniform Series." *Adult Leadership* 7/6 (March 1977): 31–35.

"Planning for Bible Study—Convention Uniform Series." *Adult Leadership* 7/7 (April 1977): 30–34.

"Studies in 1 and 2 Timothy" (eleven Sunday school lessons for 17 April–26 June 1977). *Adult Bible Study* 7/3 (April–June 1977): 18–80.

"Studies in 1 and 2 Timothy" (reprinted from *Adult Bible Study* above). *Bible Study Pocket Commentary* 10/3 (April–June 1977): 16–74.

"Faith in Action (James)" (lessons for May 1977). *Sunday School Youth B* 7/3 (April–June 1977): 25–48.

"Plan 1 Procedures." *The Youth Teacher* 7/3 (April–June 1977): 37–38, 42–43, 47–48, 53–54, 58–59.

"Item 4A-B. Faith in Action" and "Item 5A-C. Tree of Life." *Youth Teacher Resource Kit* 4/3 (April–June 1977).

"Applying the Bible Passages" (for SS lessons 1–22 July 1979). *Adult Life and Work Lesson Annual, 1978–1979*. Nashville: Convention Press, 1978. 320–21, 329–30, 337–38, 345–46.

"Special Helpers of Jesus." *VBS Teacher's Guide for Use with Middle Children*. Church series. Nashville: Convention Press, 1979.

Children Ages 6-11 Vacation Bible School Teacher. With Margie Kinard Clark. Nashville: Broadman Press, 1979.

(lesson plans). *Adult Teacher* (January–June 1982).

"Planning to Use CUS" *Adult Leadership* (April 1982).

"Department Periods." *Adult Leadership* (May 1982).

Four lesson applications in *Adult Life and Work Lesson Annual, 1982–1983*. Nashville: Convention Press, 1982.

"Relating with God," "Relating with Yourself," "Relating with Others," and "Relating with Your World." *Formations Commentary* 1/1 (September–December 1992).

"Unity in Human Relationships" (five SS lessons for April 2000). *Uniform Bible Study Series: Study Guide* 1/1 (January–April 2000): 83–112.

"Unity in Human Relationships" (five SS lessons for April 2000). *Uniform Bible Study Series: Teaching Guide* 1/1 (January–April 2000): 94–128.

Poem

"Nothing in my hand..." *Encounter. a Youth Worship Guide* 4/1 (October 1975): 51.

Review Articles

"The General and Some Latter-Day Lieutenants." *Beethoven: Biography of a Genius* (1969) by George R. Marek, and *Composers of Tomorrow's Music: A Nontechnical Introduction to the Avant-Garde Movement* (1971) by David Ewen. *The Averett Journal* 4/2 (August 1973): 73–76.

"What the Scripture Writers Meant?" *The Living Bible. Paraphrased* (1971). *The Christian Century* 91/40 (20 November 1974): 1104–106.

[Untitled.] *Theological Dictionary of the New Testament* (Volumes 1–9). *Search* 6/3 (Spring 1976): 60–64.

"Was It So True?" *So It Was True. The American Protestant Press and the Nazi Persecution of the Jews* (1980) by Robert W. Ross. *Perspectives in Religious Studies* 10/2 (Summer 1983): 175–80.

"So It Was True..." *So It Was True. The American Protestant Press and the Nazi Persecution of the Jews* (1980) by Robert W. Ross. *Search* 13/4 (Summer 1983): 54–58.

[Untitled.] *Out of the Desert? Archaeology and the Exodus/Conquest Narratives* (1989) by William H. Stiebing,

Jr. *Perspectives in Religious Studies* 18/2 (Summer 1991): 182–85.

Book Reviews

Paul by Günther Bornkamm. *The Averett Journal* 3/2 (Fall 1972): 52–55.

"The Right Question." Review of *Understanding Speaking in Tongues* by Watson E. Mills. *Christianity Today* 17/2 (27 October 1972): 21–22.

"A Theological Watchword." Review of *Beyond Cynicism: The Practice of Hope* by David Woodyard. *Christianity Today* 17/12 (16 March 1973): 34–35; and *Search* 4/1 (Fall 1973): 64–65.

Christian Reader's Guide to the Old Testament by David Yohn. *Search* 4/1 (Fall 1973): 60.

"Glad to Have Both." Review of *The Gospel According to Luke* by Anthony Lee Ash, and *Commentary on Luke. Jesus, the Universal Savior* by Ray Summers. *Christianity Today* 17/23 (31 August 1973): 31–34.

Colossians. The Church's Lord and the Christian's Liberty: An Expository Commentary with a Present-Day Application by Ralph P. Martin. *Perspectives in Religious Studies* 1/1 (Spring 1974): 93–96; and *Christianity Today* 18/5 (7 December 1973): 41–42.

The City and the Sign by Geoffrey T. Bull. *Search* 4/2 (Winter 1974): 62–63.

Contemporary Christian Trends, edited by Wm M. Pinson, Jr. and Clyde E. Fant, Jr. *Lutheran Quarterly* 25/4 (November 1973): 412–14; and *Search* 4/3 (Spring 1974): 57–58.

Christianity Without Walls by Morris Inch. *Search* 4/4 (Summer 1974): 52–53.

Moses, the Servant of Yahweh by Dewey M. Beegle. *Search* 4/4 (Summer 1974): 53–54.

Bible Comparatives by R. Earle Allen. *Search* 4/4 (Summer 1974): 54.

The Church and Her Walls: Twentieth-Century Parallels from the Book of Revelation by Daniel Kolke. *Search* 4/4 (Summer 1974): 54–55

Communication in Pulpit and Parish by Merrill R. Abbey. *Search* 5/1 (Fall 1974): 62.

The Salvation Tree by John Killinger. *Search* 5/2 (Winter 1975): 64–65.

Experimental Preaching by John Killinger. *Search* 5/2 (Winter 1975): 65–66.

The Fire Flares Anew: A Look at the New Pentecostalism by John Stevens Kerr. *Lutheran Quarterly* 26/4 (November 1974): 466–67.

Christian Counter Culture by Chester A. Pennington. *Search* 5/3 (Spring 1975): 62–63.

Multiplying the Witness by Lawrence T. Slaght. *Search* 5/3 (Spring 1975): 63–64.

Baptists, the Passionate People by C. Burtt Potter. *Search* 5/3 (Spring 1975): 65.

Introduction to the Bible by Donald J. Selby and James King West. *Search* 10/1 (Fall 1979): 65–66.

Exodus by John Durham, Word Biblical Comm. 3. *Religious Studies Review* 14/4 (October 1988): 372.

Mark: A New Translation with Introduction and Commentary by C. S. Mann, Anchor Bible 27. *Religious Studies Review* 14/4 (October 1988): 380.

John by George R. Beasley-Murray, WBC 36. *Religious Studies Review* 14/4 (October 1988): 381.

Religions of Antiquity, edited by Robert M. Seltzer, *Religion, History, and Culture*. Selections from the *Encyclopedia of Religion* (1989). *Religious Studies Review* 17/1 (January 1991): 63.

The World of Ancient Israel: Sociological, Anthropological, and Political Perspectives. Essays by Members of the Society for O.T. Study, edited by Ronald E. Clements. *Religious Studies Review* 17/3 (July 1991): 250.